INTRODUCTION

At the time of writing, there are more than two million freelancers in the UK alone, with a large percentage of those working within the creative industries. According to Simply Business, that number is increasing faster than ever before and the trend doesn't appear to be slowing down. With technology evolving at an alarming rate, it's easier than ever to start and run a freelance business, from anywhere in the world. What used to take hours to create, using expensive software, can now be done in minutes, with a free app on your phone. Technology has also opened the door to a global market, increasing opportunity and competition simultaneously. There is no denying that the creative industries, like many others, are going through a radical transformation.

Despite this, there has never been a better time to be a freelancer or start a business, but it doesn't come without its challenges. As well as running my own freelance business for the past eight years, I've also had the privilege of coaching some incredibly talented creative professionals. From award-winning photographers, to internationally recognised designers; individuals who are at the top of their creative field.

Although they have years of industry experience and are extremely good at what they do, they often find themselves asking questions such as: How do I differentiate myself in a saturated market? How do I get my clients to understand the value of what I am offering and pay what I ask? What platforms should I be promoting myself on? How do I gain more creative control, freedom and financial security?

This book is about answering those questions and more. This isn't just another feel good, self-help, 'how to' guide for freelancers, it's much more than that. I'm inviting you to play a bigger game, to solve real problems, and to push yourself beyond what you think is possible. I'm going to show you how to build a freelance business you are proud of; one that doesn't just bring you financial security, but that also gives you creative fulfilment. I won't be talking about the latest marketing techniques or how to build your Instagram following. This isn't about tactics and tools, it's about fundamental principles and strategies that will stand the test of time. They will be as relevant in ten years, as they are today. I have used them to build my own business, as well as to help hundreds of creative freelancers to build theirs.

Before you read any further, I need you to be open to the idea that it's no longer enough to be good at what you do. Your craft and creative skills will only carry you so far. It's one thing to have mastered the art of creativity, but another to have mastered the business of creativity. The latter will open doors that you never knew existed. I would like you to let go of any preconceived ideas or negative associations that you have around business, because they are probably holding you back. I used to think business was about numbers and that it involved wearing an expensive suit and driving a BMW. That was until I met creative entrepreneurs and business owners who I had admired for years. They showed me how business could be fun and that, done well, it was the ultimate form of creative expression.

This book is a combination of my experience working in various roles within the creative industries over the past 12 years, coaching world-class creative professionals, and being mentored by entrepreneurs who have built multi-million-pound businesses. I haven't held anything back; these are my best ideas, strategies and frameworks that have allowed me, and

CREATE AND PROSPER

HOW TO FIND YOUR DREAM CLIENTS AND BUILD A FREELANCE BUSINESS YOU LOVE

Matthew Essam

First published in Great Britain in 2020

All rights reserved; no part of this book may be reproduced in any form or by any electronic or mechanical means, including information storage and retrieval systems, without written permission from the author, except for the use of brief quotations in a book review.

Copyright 2020 © by Matthew Essam

The rights of Matthew Essam to be identified as the author of this work has been asserted by him in accordance with the Copyright, Designs and Patents Act.1988

This book is sold subject to the condition that it shall not, by way of trade or otherwise, be lent, resold, hired out, or otherwise circulated without the publisher's prior consent in any form of binding or cover other than that in which it is published and without a similar condition including this condition being imposed on the subsequent purchaser.

Cover image © Essam Consulting and Coaching LTD

This book is not intended to provide personalised legal, financial, or investment advice. The Author specifically disclaims any liability, loss or risk which is incurred as a consequence, directly or indirectly, of the use and application of any contents of this work.

Table of Contents

INTRODUCTION 5
   How To Get The Most From This Book 7

CHAPTER ONE—LIFESTYLE DESIGN 9
   Security Is An Illusion 12
   It's All About Emotion 17

CHAPTER TWO—YOUR GUIDING COMPASS 20
   Vehicles Vs Values 21
   What Do You Want To Avoid? 30
   Uncovering Your Emotional Formula 33
   Changing Your Formula 35

CHAPTER THREE—MAKING YOUR VALUES VALUABLE 39
   Under The Iceberg 44
   Finding Your Niche 49
   Defining Your Why 53

CHAPTER FOUR—FINDING YOUR DREAM CLIENTS 56
   Be Aspirational 59
   The Red Rope 67

CHAPTER FIVE—ACTIVE VS PASSIVE 69
   Meaningful Conversations 72
   Start At The Beginning 74

CHAPTER SIX—STARTING MEANINGFUL
CONVERSATIONS 77
   The Power Is In The Pitch 79
   Don't Propose On The First Date 82
   The Logical Next Step 85
   C.A.M.P.S. 88

CHAPTER SEVEN—HOW TO SELL WITHOUT FEELING
SALESY 92
   Reframing Sales 94
   What Do They Really Want? 97
   The Two Islands 98

Becoming The Guide 101

CHAPTER EIGHT—STOP SELLING YOUR TIME 104
    Sell Them What They Want, Give Them What They Need 105
    Building Your Offer 109
    Features Vs Benefits 110
    Creating A Collective 111
    How Much Should You Charge? 112
    Feedback, Not Failure 114
    Customer To Client 115

CHAPTER NINE—YOU CAN'T DO IT ALONE 119
    Letting Go Of Control 122
    Automation, Delegation And Elimination 124
    Creating Systems 126

CHAPTER TEN—NUGGETS OF WISDOM 129
    Discomfort Is The Gateway To Success 130
    Someone, Somewhere Woke Up Today With Exactly
    What You Need 132
    There Is No Such Thing As The Right Time. 133
    Fit Your Oxygen Mask First 133
    It's Hard And It Gets Harder 134
    You Are More Powerful Than You Think 135
    Afterword 137
    What next? 138
    Acknowledgements 140
    About Matthew Essam 141

many of my clients, to create an extraordinary quality of life on our terms.

How To Get The Most From This Book

I have written this book in a way that allows you to dive into each chapter individually and find strategies that you can apply to your life and business straight away. However, if you really want to take things to the next level, I advise that you read it from start to finish, several times. The books that have had the most impact on my life are the ones with dog-eared pages, battered and broken from use. The first chapters are as important as the last. It's a little bit like a recipe book, you could probably make something that tastes ok from picking out certain ingredients, but if you want to create a four-course meal, you need to include everything, and in the right order.

If you are at a point in your career where you are still honing your craft and building up to working with commercial clients, it probably isn't the best time to be reading this book. Focus on getting good at your skill or craft and then come back and read this. However, if you have been freelancing for a while, but still feel something is missing, this book was written for you.

If you just read this for entertainment and don't do anything with the insights, nothing will change. Throughout the book, I have included exercises and provided links to bonus material, to help you implement the insights into your own life and business. If you don't take any action, then reading this book will be a waste of your valuable time. If you know that you are the kind of person who has the tendency not to act on insights, then there are plenty of opportunities to get help. I was guilty of this in the early years of my career. I thought that if I knew all of the best business strategies, I would suddenly wake up with a successful business. When I realised that wasn't going to make it happen, I became committed to surrounding myself with people who would push me to implement and test those ideas, not to just learn the theory.

You can't pass your driving test on theory alone; you have to get out there and learn to drive. This book has some powerful tools and strategies that can transform your life and business, but you have to take them for a spin. In the coming chapters, I will be walking you through the exact process I use with my clients to help them get unstuck and achieve their goals. I'm sure you are eager to know what they are, so let's get started.

CHAPTER ONE
LIFESTYLE DESIGN

> "Success without fulfillment is the ultimate failure." - Anthony Robbins

It was 1pm on a Tuesday afternoon and I had a strange sinking feeling in my stomach. As I sat on the powdery snow, overlooking the hazy mountains, I couldn't shake the feeling that something wasn't right. I had spent the last two years working for moments just like this, but it felt as empty and cold as the snow beneath me.

Three months prior to this, I had travelled to five countries over three continents, having built a freelance business that I could run from anywhere in the world. My Instagram feed was filled with photos that would make regular jet setters envious, and from the outside, it looked like I had the perfect life. I felt guilty for not being entirely happy, as I knew a lot of people would give anything to be in my shoes, but I also knew something had to change.

Sometimes we get so caught up in our own story that we need an external event to help us shift our perspective and create that change. For me, that came in the form of a sudden, tragic death in my family. As Baz Luhrmann famously said in his song, Sunscreen, "The real troubles in your life are apt to be things that never crossed your worried mind, the kind that blindside you at 4 p.m. on some idle Tuesday". As I sat looking out of the aeroplane window, wondering what my family back in England must be feeling, I started to see the world from a completely different perspective.

Whether you have experienced a tragedy in your life or not, there will have been times when you have felt this shift for yourself. As painful as that event was to experience, it was also a gift in disguise. It was a sharp reminder of the fleeting time that we have on this beautiful planet. A reminder not to take anything for granted and not to sweat the small stuff. To follow your heart and do something that makes you come alive, but most importantly, it's a reminder of what really matters.

It took awhile for the cloud of emotions to settle down enough for me to make any of these links, but when it did, I began to question everything. Was I really doing what I wanted with my life? Why were these goals I had achieved not making me feel the way I wanted? I had everything most people would ever want, so why wasn't I happy?

On the verge of an existential crisis, I frantically searched for answers. From TED talks, to self-help books, I consumed as much information as possible in an attempt to find a theory or a strategy that would help me to gain some clarity and reassurance. The one thing that kept coming up as I was on this journey was an overwhelming feeling that nothing I did really mattered. If I stopped designing websites and creating logos for people tomorrow, they would just find someone else to do it. This realisation was accompanied by a rising sense of anxiety as I started to develop a nihilistic outlook on life. I realised that if I wanted to feel a sense of true fulfilment, I needed to find something bigger than myself to put my energy into. But what was that thing and how did I go about finding it?

I spent months navel-gazing and being introspective, in the hope that I would eventually discover my new sense of purpose. It was frustrating and exhausting. I read book after book and watched countless videos that emphasised the importance of having a purpose, but most seemed to lack a practical explanation of exactly how to find it!

One day, down a deep YouTube rabbit hole, I came across a short TED talk about the Japanese word 'ikigai', which roughly translates to "reason for being", or why you get out of bed in the morning. The Japanese believe that everyone has an 'ikigai' and the secret to a long, happy, fulfilling life is to find yours and live by it. This wasn't news to me, but when I Googled the word to find out more, I came across a diagram that changed everything.

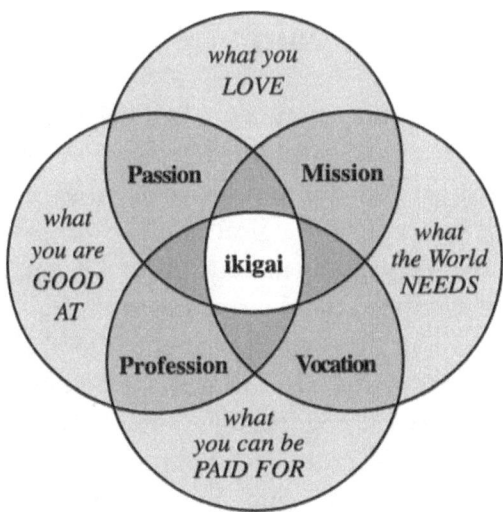

Diagram originally created by British community activist, Marc Winn, in 2014.

I realised that, despite spending years at school, studying subjects I didn't like, despite going to university and graduating with a good degree, despite being self-employed and having the freedom to do what I wanted, I was still firmly in the 'profession' box. In other words, I just had a job that I could do from anywhere in the world. That may sound exotic, but there are only a certain number of cocktails and beaches that can distract you from the reality that you don't enjoy what you are doing for a living. Eventually, it all starts to feel a bit meaningless. I love travelling and I think everyone should experience as much of it as possible, but for me, it wasn't the secret to finding true fulfilment. So, what was keeping me from doing what I really loved and setting the world on fire? When I really thought about that question, I realised that any time I had followed my passion, I had never really been able to make things work financially. I wanted the security of a permanent job, but the freedom of being a freelancer.

Security Is An Illusion

I had a sudden realisation that I had been playing it safe. It certainly didn't feel safe, but I knew I was doing the things that I knew I could get paid for and focusing on skills that were in demand. This seems like a logical thing to do as a freelancer, and it did serve me well, financially, up to a point. However, it meant I often sacrificed the things I was really passionate about to earn money. I'm sure you've experienced this at times in your life and most people refer to it as 'bread-and-butter work' – the work we take on because it pays the bills or projects that are boring, but look great on the portfolio. These are all attempts to create security and financial stability in our life, something we all need. If we aren't careful though, it's not long before we have low paying projects from clients that have unrealistic expectations. We get bogged down, stressed out and overworked, all because we believe it's the safer option.

The problem is that security is based less on reality and more on our perception. One person's idea of security is another person's idea of total uncertainty. Most of us have been conditioned to believe that having a steady job, a house and a good pension are the ultimate forms of security. In psychology, this is referred to as cognitive bias, and unfortunately, we are all susceptible to it. Let's say you believe that people who are left-handed are more creative than people who are right-handed. When you meet someone who is both left-handed and creative, this will reinforce your belief. In fact, if we looked at the evidence objectively, there would be little to support this belief. In relation to security, this cognitive bias is easily observed in fears and phobias such as flying. I went through a period where I hated flying and whenever there was turbulence, I would grip the arm rest for dear life. I knew the odds of dying in a plane crash were extremely low, but that didn't change my perception or belief about that event in that moment.

Jim Carrey shares a beautiful anecdote during his famous commencement speech at Maharishi International University in Iowa, which demonstrates how the illusion of security can have a significant impact on our lives. He tells the story of his father who always wanted to be a comedian, but he trained to be an accountant instead, as he thought it was a safer option. When Jim was 12 years old, his father was fired from his secure job, leaving his family in serious financial difficulty. Carrey then goes on to say that because of this, he learnt at an early age that "you can fail at what you don't want, so you might as well take a chance doing what you love."

I'm not suggesting you just throw everything out of the window and follow your lifelong dream to be a surf instructor in Bali (although that would be cool). Nor am I saying that having bigger clients on your portfolio doesn't make it easier to attract other big clients. My point is simply that security is an illusion and by prioritising it, we are often left in a place where we have regrets, and when things don't work out, it becomes a much harder pill to swallow.

It reminds me of when I started a record label in my mid-twenties. From the beginning, my co-founder and I agreed that no matter what happened, we would always release music we both loved; we didn't want a catalogue of music that neither of us wanted to listen to. We both knew what was selling in certain genres and we could quite easily have jumped on that bandwagon. It's easy to think that it would have increased our chances of success, but neither of us really liked that kind of music, so we decided to only release music that we would buy ourselves. Although the label didn't allow us to retire early, we did have a few songs that got some fairly large exposure, as well as having a record of the week chosen for BBC six music. I can look back on that venture with pride and lots of valuable lessons.

My point here is that if you're going to fail (which we all do at some point), make sure it's with something you really care about. Something that makes your heart sing. Life is too short to settle. The world needs people willing to dream big and solve meaningful problems. We have a much higher chance of succeeding when doing something we are deeply passionate about, rather than just following a path for the sole reason that it pays the bills.

The challenge of course is that we do have to pay the bills. It's not enough just to do something you are passionate about. If it were, then I'm sure there would be far more surf instructors in Bali. When you have a family to support, paying the bills is often a higher priority than doing something you love, but I'm going to show you how security and passion aren't mutually exclusive. We can have passion, excitement and fulfilment, whilst achieving financial security.

I used to joke with my friend that freelance projects usually fell into one of two categories. The first was fun, creatively fulfilling and meaningful, but never had a big budget. The second was well paid but was mostly unfulfilling and monotonous. Every now and again, I would stumble across projects that were the best of both categories: creatively fulfilling and well paid! I used to refer to this as the elusive third category of work. The frustrating thing was, I could never figure out how to find those projects consistently. I tried adding bigger brands to my portfolio and posting my work on social media, but it just seemed to gain attention and respect from other creative freelancers, rather than my dream clients.

I came to accept that this was just how the creative industry works. You have your bread-and-butter work and then you can be a bit choosier with some of the other projects that come in.

That was until I came across several freelancers and small agencies that seemed to only be involved with the third category of work. All of a sudden, I had this burning desire to find out what they were doing differently, in the hope I would uncover some sort of secret formula.

I set about contacting everyone I knew who seemed to be doing this third category of work, to see if I could meet up with them and ask questions. I'm not sure if you've ever tried this, but in general, people aren't too keen to divulge the inner workings of their business to someone they don't know that well. I did manage to have a few conversations with agency owners and freelancers I admired, but often, they gave fairly generic advice in relation to their success such as hard work and passion. The problem was, I knew plenty of people who were hard working and passionate but didn't have the same level of success. It became apparent that If I wanted to build a business that allowed me to work with clients I loved, earn what I wanted and work on projects I was proud of, I was going to have to invest a significant amount of time and money.

When I started this search, there seemed to be a lot less "gurus" out there than there are today. I had read 20 or 30 good business books, so I had some ideas about strategy, but I needed help with the implementation. What should I be focusing on now? Does this apply to me, and will it get me to where I want to be?

Over the next few years, I would invest hundreds of hours, tens of thousands of pounds and every last bit of energy I had into finding the answers to these questions. I painstakingly tried and tested every last bit of advice I got, until I found something that started to create tangible results. Within the first year, I had changed my business drastically. I terminated work with 80% of my clients, created a brand-new offering and doubled my income. Since then, I've been continually testing and refining these strategies to develop a framework that I can use with all of my clients. From designers to stone masons, these principles and strategies apply to service-based businesses throughout the creative and digital sector. I'm not claiming to have all of the answers or be an expert, in fact, I believe you are the expert and my job is to help you see your life and business in a different way; to help you focus on the things that matter and give you the life and business you really want.

Over the coming chapters, I'm going to be sharing the 20% of ideas and strategies that have created 80% of results for me and my clients. To start with, I want you to think about two questions that most people completely ignore on this journey: what do you really want, and why do you want it? I know you'd probably like me to just get to the juicy part and tell you how to win higher value clients and do more of the work you love. I get that, I've been there. We just want things to work and are maybe a bit tired of reading endless amounts of books or blogs and not getting any closer to the answer. But what if I told you that these two questions are two of **the most important** and **most powerful** questions you can ask yourself? Remember the story I told at the beginning of this chapter? Well, that was a result of not spending enough time asking myself those two questions and I don't want you to fall into the same trap.

It's easy to get caught up in the logistics of what projects you want to work on or what new skills you want to learn and lose sight of the bigger picture. For example, you might think that you will be content when you work with a specific brand or client, or when you get to the point where you don't have to worry if you have enough money in your account to cover the bills. In my experience, those factors only play a small part in the overall picture. I say this not only from my own experience, but from working with very successful freelancers and creative agencies who had all of those things and still weren't happy. The truth is, it's less about *what* you want and more about *why* you want it. In other words, how do you want to feel?

It's All About Emotion

If someone asked you why you went freelance or started a business, you could probably list quite a few reasons. It might be because you didn't enjoy working for someone else or you wanted a better work-life balance. Some people want to spend more time with their children and have the flexibility to work when and where they want. But what would you say if someone asked you *why* you want those things?

I would be willing to bet that if you were asked that question enough times, your answer would boil down to an emotion. You may say something like "because it gives me a sense of freedom" or "I want to feel like I'm in control of when and where I work". Whatever your answer, it's rarely the logistical or material things you actually desire. That was what really stumped me about my situation. I had a freelance business that I could run from anywhere in the world and was working when and where I wanted, but I didn't *feel* free. It wasn't just because I was constantly searching for a good Wi-Fi connection or had to take calls at strange times of the day. It was this underlying sense that, although I could be anywhere in the world, I still felt trapped.

Have you ever achieved a goal you spent ages working towards and not been any happier when you actually achieved it? Maybe you were happy and excited for a while, but that soon wore off and you started looking for the next thing? It's a hard pill to swallow when you get the things you want, but you still aren't happy and fulfilled. In fact, it's one of the scenarios that causes many people to be depressed or become addicted to drugs and alcohol. They are trying to find a way to add that next level to their life or numb the reality that they are unfulfilled but are going the wrong way about it.

Let's go back to why you went freelance or started a business in the first place. Maybe you wanted to spend more time with your children or have a better work-life balance. Stop for a second and think about what those things would really give you. Is it a feeling of love and connection? Maybe it's a sense of joy and pride or freedom. When I stopped to examine all of the goals and dreams I had, I realised it was actually an emotion that I wanted, not the goal itself. I wanted to feel a sense of **freedom, respect** and **significance.** I wanted to feel **connected** and be able to express myself creatively. When

I *really* thought about these things, it was clear that the lifestyle I had manufactured wasn't going to give me those feelings on a consistent basis.

I had created too many rules around these emotions and had a huge list of criteria that had to be met before I gave myself permission to experience them.

For example, my criteria for freedom was that I had to be able to travel the world when I wanted, not have to answer to anyone, be able to choose exactly when I worked…and the list went on. I suddenly realised I was so focused on my goals that I had completely neglected my values.

CHAPTER TWO
YOUR GUIDING COMPASS

> "It's not hard to make decisions when you know what your values are."
> - Roy Disney

When you hear the word 'values', you might think of things like honesty and integrity, or fairness and equality. I have no doubt those are things you value, but I would like you to think about values slightly differently for the purpose of this chapter. What about, instead of thinking of values as a set of words or phrases, we thought about them as emotional states? The things we want to feel, or don't want to feel, on a daily basis.

For example, you may say that honesty and integrity is one of your highest values but think about how often you experience feelings of honesty and integrity. Is it something you value or something you feel? There is a big difference. Have you ever found yourself saying something like, "if I could get this client, then I would be happy" or "if I could just earn this much per year, my life would be amazing". Whenever we find ourselves having these thoughts, we must acknowledge that we are focusing on the thing we think is going to bring us that emotion, rather than the emotion itself. I refer to this distinction as the vehicle and the value.

Vehicles Vs Values

Our goals are the vehicles, and the emotions are the values. The vehicle is the thing we think will give us the emotion, and the value is the emotion itself. When I first start working with a client, I ask them what their ultimate dream is. They might say something like having their photos displayed in the most prestigious galleries in the world or creating a film that becomes a cult classic. When they are telling me, I'm listening for the emotion behind the dream or goal. In this case, it might be 'significance' or 'respect'. It might be to leave a legacy so that they are remembered. Either way, if we don't *feel* those things, we won't get the same level of satisfaction and fulfilment from the result.

Imagine for a moment that you have achieved your wildest dreams and everything you have ever wanted has come true, but you still lack a sense of fulfilment and achievement. How would that make you feel? I would imagine not great. So how do we make sure that doesn't happen? To begin answering this question, we first need to understand how our values are formed and where they come from. It's very difficult to change something if we don't understand how it works.

Most of us haven't consciously decided what our values are. We didn't sit down and list emotions that we want to feel or don't want to feel on a daily basis. Our values are created throughout our life, based on our experiences and interactions with the world around us. They are then reinforced by where we go to school, who we are friends with and what our parents believe to be important. This means that most of us have an unconscious system that determines the emotions we feel on a daily basis. This system runs on autopilot and rarely do we take the controls. We are conditioned to believe that if we achieve certain goals in life, they will give us certain feelings. But as you've probably experienced, this isn't always true. I believe this is exactly why we see so many successful artists rise to fame and then numb their lives with drugs and alcohol.

They have the **vehicles** (money, fame, best-selling albums etc.), but they aren't experiencing the **values** (freedom, respect, love, connection) that they thought it would give them. I've come to realise that if we want a true sense of fulfilment in our lives, we must consciously choose our values and actively decide how we are going to attain them. Don't worry, I'm going to be showing you how to achieve your goals, as well.

When I looked back at my own story, I saw that I was waiting for some day in the future when I had achieved a list of goals, before I gave myself permission to experience certain emotions. Not only did that mean I wasn't happy until that point, but those feelings never lasted long because once I had achieved that goal, I wanted to move to the next thing straight away.

The best thing about making your values conscious, is that it allows you to design a life that lets you experience those emotions **now,** rather than some day in the future. The first step to doing this is understanding what you *truly* want. This is a process that involves a bit of creative imagination and brutal honesty. Most people think about life in relation to their own world view, but this perspective is limited by our beliefs. To really understand what is important to us, we need to think about life from a different view and shift our perspective. For me, that was triggered by a series of events, but the breaking point was the death in my family. It made me think about what was really important and what I valued. Ideally, we don't want to wait for a major life event to shift our perspective, as we might be waiting a while. Luckily, we all possess an extremely powerful tool that can create a shift immediately, and it lives between our ears.

There is a part of our brain, associated with imagination, called the cerebrum, which can't identify between what is happening in real life and what is happening in our imagination. This is why you get sweaty palms and a racing heart when you watch a scary film. Our body is reacting to a perceived threat, rather than a real one. Our imagination is one of the most powerful tools in the world and it is unique to humans. So let's take five minutes to use it for something constructive that could alter the course of your life.

I'm going to ask you to imagine a scenario that will help you to think outside the constraints of social norms and remove any conditioning you have picked up over the years. It's one of the most powerful exercises that I guide my clients through, and with the risk of sounding overly dramatic, it has literally changed people's lives. If you really lean into this exercise, I promise you, you will see the power and potential of it.

Step One: The Perspective Shift

Before you do this exercise, it's best to be sitting down somewhere comfortable without any distractions. We are going to be daydreaming and it's important we aren't continually disturbed. If you aren't in a place where you can do that, then make sure you return to this exercise when you are. Don't skip it!

Imagine you've just finished a long, hard day's work and come home to find a letter on your kitchen table. It's addressed to you and marked private and confidential. You open the letter and start reading, it starts to dawn on you that you've been presented with a shocking and unique scenario. Recent blood tests show that you have a rare, incurable disease and have been given a maximum of three years to live. The disease is so rare that only a handful of people in the entire world have ever been diagnosed with it. This scenario isn't all bad though; as you continue reading, you are told that the last person to have the disease was a billionaire and before they died, they put all of their money in a foundation that supports the small handful of people who get diagnosed with this rare disease.

You have been allocated a few hundred million pounds to use, however you like, over the next three years. There will be no record given to the foundation of how the money was spent and it's free for you to enjoy. You also have access to their contact list, which contains details of some of the most influential people in the world, from Presidents to A list celebrities. You can contact any of them and ask them for a favour, you have total freedom. Take at least ten minutes to write down what you would do in those next three years. For example, where would you travel, who would you spend time with and what would you buy? Let your imagination run wild.

If you do this exercise properly, it will allow you to think beyond our ideas of what you believe is possible or what you should or shouldn't be doing. This exercise is the first step to identifying your personal values, opposed to the values of your friends, family or society.

When my clients do this exercise, they sometimes feel guilty about what they have written down. For example, one client said all he could think about doing was taking drugs, going to heavy metal concerts and smashing things up. He also felt guilty that his family weren't involved in all of the imaginary scenarios. I encouraged him to imagine this world without judgement and let his mind run wild. It's important you don't worry about what you believe you *should* be doing and just focus on what you really want. Imagine no one will see this and no one will judge any of your actions.

Once people get into the flow of this exercise, they can often write huge paragraphs on where they would travel, who they would spend time with and what they would do. From this, I can immediately start to see some of their core values. After completing this exercise, you will find yourself with a list of everything you would possibly do, have, or create. In other words, a list of vehicles. The ways in which you believe you will get certain values met.

Step Two: Uncovering The Value

Out of everything you have written down, I want you to look for common themes. For example, one theme could be travel. Another may be spending time with family or donating things to charity (don't worry if none of those things came up). Once you've found the themes, ask yourself *why* you really want those things. What emotion/s are you hoping they will give you?

People often find this question difficult to answer. If they answer straight away, it's usually with a surface level statement such as "it would make me happy" or "because I would be successful". The important part of this process is to dig down below the surface and think about the emotion you are really hoping to feel by having/ doing all of those things. For my client who wanted to take lots of drugs, listen to heavy metal music and smash things up, we explored why he wanted to do this and found that those things would allow him to let go of all responsibility and just do what he wanted. In other words, he wanted a sense of **freedom.**

For myself, and many of my clients, freedom and variety are linked to travel. However, it was the experience of travelling but **not** feeling freedom that allowed me to realise it was a vehicle, not a value. It also allowed me to see that if travel was the only vehicle that I had linked to freedom, I would either have to be a nomad for the rest of my life or be unhappy. This is true for most things we desire, such as money, relationships, success etc.

They are all vehicles for an emotion that we are craving, which we believe is important for us to experience. For each vehicle or theme you have written down, your aim is to uncover the emotion linked to it. The easiest way I have found to do this, is to simply ask why? Why do I want this, why is it important to me? You will know you have reached a value when the answer to that question is phrased in relation to an emotion. For example "it will give me a sense of freedom" or "It will make me feel like I'm making a difference".

Now take five to ten minutes to write down all of the emotions that are linked to the vehicles you have identified.

Notes

Once we have uncovered our values, we need to work out which ones are the most important to us. We all share similar values, but it's to what extent. Let's look at this in Step Three: The Order Of Importance.

In front of you should be a list of emotions that you believe are important for you to experience. The question now becomes, which ones are the **most** important?

For example, is it more important to feel a sense of freedom or respect?

The reason why we are identifying the order of importance is because it will dictate everything you do in life. When I know the order or someone's values, I can start to understand why they do certain things and why they might be a bit stuck. In fact, feeling stuck is usually just a sign that there is a conflict in someone's values. For example, we might want freedom, but we also want security. Or we might want love and connection but hate the feeling of rejection (we will talk more about negative emotions shortly).

As you can probably imagine, someone whose number one value is security, is going to live life differently to someone that has freedom as their most important value. When you can get your values and their hierarchy from your head on to paper, you have the power to change your life. This exercise may take you a bit longer, but I want you to list the top five values in order of importance.

The top five emotions I want to feel in order of importance are:

1.
2.
3.
4.
5.

At this point, I wouldn't be surprised if you were wondering what this all has to do with running a freelance business. The short answer is that we are building a business from our life, rather than a life from our business.

I promise, you will understand the relevance in the next few chapters and see that by getting clear on your values, it will allow you to have more of what you want on a daily basis, in spite of what is happening in your business logistically. Let me give you an example of what the above exercise looked like when I first did it (I've intentionally shortened my answers for the purpose of this book).

If you were told tomorrow that you only had three years to live, but you had an unlimited amount of money, what would you do?

"I would travel the world and experience new things, whilst connecting and adding value to as many people's lives as possible. I would attend all of the best courses and seminars in the world…"

Why would you do that? Why is it important to you?

I love to travel because of the freedom it gives me. It would make me feel as though I was making the most of my time on the planet by experiencing lots of new things. I would feel as though I was making a difference and contributing beyond myself and creating value within society. I would feel as though I am continually learning and growing as a person. Acquiring the best strategies and frameworks so I could help more people and have a bigger impact.

What emotions can you identify from this exercise?

Freedom

Variety / exploration Making a difference Learning

Growth

What is more important for you to experience?

1: Making a difference 2: Variety / exploration 3: Freedom

4: Learning

5: Growth

Interestingly, I found that, although travel was important, as it gave me a sense of freedom and variety, I valued making a difference the most. The recent events in my life had made me realise that if I was just travelling the world and having new experiences, I would lack true fulfilment.

So I promised I would tell you how this all linked to running a freelance business...

If you imagine your values are like a compass, they can guide you through life, help you to evaluate situations and make better decisions. When I first start working with my clients, they often tell me they feel stuck and can't decide where to focus their time and energy. They are usually trying to imagine every possible scenario in their head before they make a decision and are so focused on the logistics of the situation, they forget about the values.

For example, one of my clients, Steve, was really struggling to decide how to position himself as a photographer. He had done a wide range of work over the years, from weddings, to travel photography, and couldn't decide which direction to take moving forwards. He had so many questions flying around in his head like; how should I present my portfolio? Do I even want to do weddings anymore? How will I pay the bills if I drop certain things? As you've probably experienced in your own life, these kinds of questions create uncertainty, which, if left unchecked, can undermine your confidence and self-belief. Steve's assumption was that the answer to these questions was a logistical one, instead of an emotional one. When I asked him how he wanted to feel on a daily basis and started to uncover his values, he suddenly had a breakthrough.

Steve now has a "guiding path" in his own words. A clear direction that allows him to let go of the things outside of his control and build a business from the inside out. Over the last few years, I've had the privilege of working with some very successful entrepreneurs and creative business owners. One of the things I quickly noticed about them was that they all made decisions quickly and had an unshakable confidence, no matter what was happening in their life and business. After having some fairly lengthy discussions with many of them, it was obvious that they operated in the same way and had an internal filter that they ran everything through, consciously. It suddenly made sense why they appeared so calm all of the time; they had a guiding path that they were following and knew any setbacks were only temporary. If we use our values to make decisions, rather than endlessly analysing the logistics, life becomes so much easier.

What Do You Want To Avoid?

If we think of values as emotional states, there are two types we can experience: negative and positive. At a basic level, our brain is simply trying to move us away from danger and towards safety. Said in an emotional context, towards pleasure and away from pain. Values are simply the way we express these feelings in greater detail. Our negative values work in the exact same way as our positive ones. Although I'm not going to ask you to go through the entire exercise again, I do want you to be aware that they can influence each other.

For example, someone may have significance or respect as their number one positive value but hate feeling judged or rejected. You may value freedom and autonomy but hate uncertainty or change. Is it likely that you will be able to experience one without the other? A lot of people I speak to seem to want the security of a 9-5 salary, with the freedom of running their own freelance business. Although there are some companies out there who have managed to replicate this, in general, if you are a freelancer or small business owner, life is much easier if you embrace uncertainty. Think of negative and positive values like the accelerator and brake in a car. If you are pushing them both at the same time, you aren't going to move anywhere.

These conflicts tend to be subconscious and can usually be described as a part of you that wants to do one thing, whilst another part wants to do something else. This is what I refer to as a 'values conflict'. So what happens if we identify a conflict of values? Firstly, congratulations, you've identified patterns that are probably causing you some stress and frustration in your life. Not only that, but these conflicts will be stopping you from reaching your full potential. Most people will go through their entire lives without discovering this. The hardest part is making these values conscious.

In order to resolve these conflicts, we need to look at your 'emotional formula'. This formula has been created and reinforced at certain points throughout your life and tells your brain when to feel certain emotions. It may seem like emotions are controlled by external events, but in fact, *we* create them. When I first discovered this concept, I struggled to get my head around it. I was so used to external events dictating how I felt that I couldn't process the concept that I was actually creating them. Now that I understand and accept the concept, I see it almost every day (some situations being more obvious than others). The event that helped me to understand this process more clearly was when watching a football match.

I had travelled down to London to watch a football team I've followed since I was about eight years old. They were in the playoff finals against a long-standing rival and the winner would be promoted to the next league. The stadium was filled to the rooftops with more than 75,000 people who had come to watch the game from far and wide and the atmosphere was electric. The game started off at a fast pace, but before I even sat down, I found myself doing a double take and my heart sank into my stomach. What seemed like a simple pass back to the goalkeeper, turned out to be a completely misread pass and the ball was slowly heading for the back of my team's net. The keeper scrambled after the ball, but it was too late. It had already crossed the line and a wave of sound erupted from the opposite end of the stadium as the rival fans celebrated.

At that moment, there were a variety of emotions being experienced by everyone in the ground. Some of our fans were sitting with their heads in their hands, looking like they had just been told they only had a few months to live. Others were bemused and seemed like they hadn't fully processed the event. Some people were standing up, encouraging everyone to keep singing and get behind the team, and at the opposite end of the stadium, the opposing fans were laughing, singing and celebrating.

All of these different emotions had been created by the **exact** same event. The simple act of the ball crossing the line had caused thousands of people to feel completely contrasting emotions, in the space of a few seconds. You may think that people have different personalities and therefore react in different ways, but the truth is, we have been conditioned to feel those things. We have a default pattern that we run when certain events happen externally and it's our emotional formula that determines how we feel about those events.

So what does this have to do with running a freelance business? Well let's go back to the analogy of driving a car; if I give you a Ferrari, but you drive it around with one foot on the accelerator and one on the break, you aren't going to move very fast. In fact, you would probably blow up the engine. The strategies and principles I'm sharing with you throughout this book will be useless if you have conflicting values or an emotional formula that is keeping you stuck. Having read hundreds of business and self-help books and spent tens of thousands of pounds attending workshops and seminars, I've realised that implementation is the real secret to success. An average strategy with great implementation is a hundred times better than a perfect strategy with little or no implementation.

In the next section, I'm going to show you how to uncover your emotional formula and create a new one so that you can get out of your own way and start making the impact you really want with your work. If you ever feel you are holding yourself back or have a feeling that no matter what you achieve, you are never quite content, this exercise is a great way to figure out exactly why that is.

Uncovering Your Emotional Formula

Each of us has an emotional formula that we carry around (usually subconsciously). It is typically created when we are children and reinforced or reordered through significant emotional events in our life. Think of it like a maths formula, in our head we have something that looks a bit like this:

If I do X, I will get Y, which will make me feel Z. Or, if X happens, it means Y, which makes me feel Z.

For example, if I "work hard", I will "earn lots of money", which will make me feel "significant".

We tend to identify with this formula so strongly that it defines who we are. For example, you might say I'm not a controversial person or I'm a people-pleaser. What you really mean is that you have a formula that says: "If I confront someone, it means they will dislike me, which makes me feel worthless".

Problems arise when we aren't aware of our emotional formula. When we merge our identity with these formulas, they become an intrinsic part of who we believe we are. Ultimately, this means that a lot of the things we achieve in our life, or business, won't make us happy. As we discovered earlier, we can have all of the material things in the world, but if we are angry, frustrated or depressed most of the time, what use are they? The quality of our life really is determined by the quality of our emotions.

When I was reflecting on my own journey, trying to understand why I felt so unfulfilled and empty, I realised I had a formula that made it almost impossible for me to experience my values. In order to feel a sense of freedom, I had to be travelling the world, not being told what to do, being able to pick and choose when I worked, the list was almost endless. I had so many things that needed to happen before I gave myself permission to experience that emotion. In contrast, imagine what formula someone might have for freedom if they had just been released from prison. It would probably be something like, "I feel freedom anytime I'm not locked up in a cell!". If that was your formula, you would feel freedom every day. They are in the exact same environment as you, experiencing the same things externally, but feeling completely different internally. The good news is, we can choose our formula and make it easier for us to meet our values on a daily basis.

When I first realised this, it felt a little bit like cheating. I thought that if I designed my life to make it easy for me to feel these emotions, I would lose my drive. I imagined myself being happy, sitting on my sofa watching Netflix all day. Luckily, through trial and error, I worked out that there was a way to use my values and formula to create more drive, motivation and energy. I still had goals, ambitions and dreams, but they were now an amplification of the values I wanted to feel every day, rather than having to achieve those goals before ever feeling those emotions.

Changing Your Formula

You may have noticed, with the earlier example at the football stadium, our interpretation of external events is created by the meaning we give to them. Therefore, if we want to change our emotional formula to make it easier to feel our positive values, and harder to experience our negative values, we first have to look at the meaning attached to each value. When I looked at my formula, it was clear that I had a strong sense of meaning around travel and, in my mind, freedom meant the ability to travel anytime I wanted, without having to answer to anyone, anywhere in the world. Not only was it a specific formula, but it was also very difficult to achieve. If even one of those things wasn't quite right, I felt like I had failed to achieve a sense of freedom.

I then asked myself what else freedom could mean. What are some other times in my life I have experienced freedom? I started to create a list of alternative things I could do that would also give me a sense of freedom. It didn't mean I had to give up my goal of travelling, it just meant that I could start experiencing freedom today. I realised that I would have a much better chance of achieving my goals if I was already experiencing these emotions, rather than experiencing negative emotions consistently. The idea here is to give yourself as much choice as possible for your positive values and restricted choice for your negative ones.

Here is an example of what my new formula looked like:

I feel a sense of freedom anytime I... Can plan my own day

Decide what project I am going to work on

Am able to take a break from work whenever I want Can travel to new places

Can choose which clients I work with Can take a day off when I choose

For my negative values, I asked myself what else these emotions could mean and started to come up with a similar list. I decided that I only wanted to feel these negative emotions when certain criteria were met. For example, I only wanted to feel rejected when I consistently allowed other people's opinions of me to become more important than my opinion of myself.

I appreciate that reading these ideas in a book can help you understand them intellectually, but you may be asking how you actually apply this to your own life. How do we just decide not to feel a certain emotion? Is that really possible?

It is if our brain realises the long-term consequences of having this formula. Remember when I said that, on a basic level, our brain wants to move us away from danger and towards safety? Well, this is why it has the emotional formula that it does. It's simply created emotional patterns so it doesn't have to analyse every situation in detail and can make life-saving decisions! The only problem is these patterns might not be serving us now or we may have picked up formula from other people. If we really want to change our emotional formula, we have to experience pain by having them in their current form. To do this, imagine what life will be like in 3, 5 and 10 years' time if you keep this formula and continue to run these patterns? What will it look like if you keep these meanings associated with your values? Just as you did when you were identifying the values, use your imagination to really experience this now.

Imagine you are grey and old, sitting in a rocking chair at the end of your life. How have these emotional formulas impacted upon what you achieved? What have they stopped you from doing? What do you regret? If you do this exercise properly, it will involve the emotional side of your brain, not just your logical side. There are lots of things we know logically make sense, but we still don't do them. Feeling is much more powerful than thinking and this is why it's so important to use our imagination to visualise these things happening. As I said earlier in the book, our emotional brain can't tell the difference between something happening in real life and something happening in our imagination.

Another way to change your criteria is to examine your beliefs about a particular emotion. For example, let's look at rejection. Some people experience the feeling of being rejected on a regular basis, whereas others hardly ever do. So why is that? Well, the person who feels it all of the time will have a different formula from someone who rarely experiences it. Two people may pitch an idea to someone, both get negative feedback and are told the idea won't work. The first person feels rejected, upset and unmotivated, while the second feels grateful, motivated and excited. The same situation, but two different reactions and emotional responses. One person may have a formula that says "anytime someone rejects an idea, it gets me closer to finding an idea that will work", whilst another person could have a formula that says "anytime someone rejects an idea, it means I'm worthless and will never succeed".

Think about the formula you currently have and ask yourself what else it could mean. When might rejection be a good thing for example? Are they really rejecting you, or are they just rejecting your idea? If two people had the same idea, can it really belong to you? What are some other ways you could look at this emotion? Just remember, this meaning was created through our experiences and what other people told us it meant (usually our parents, school, society etc.). We have the ability to change these meanings and create a new formula which will propel us towards our values and goals. Ultimately, our aim is to get to the point where we can live our values on a daily basis so that we can be happy and fulfilled in the work we do.

Now you've got a clear idea of your values and emotional formula, you will be able to drive the metaphorical car much more smoothly. This chapter isn't just about feeling great every day and walking around with a big smile on your face. It's about understanding what really drives you, the emotion behind all of your actions (and other peoples'). If you can understand this, it will help you navigate the inevitable challenges you will face on your journey. Running a freelance business isn't easy and it's made ten times harder if you are driving along with one foot on the accelerator and one on the brake.

The process we have just been through has been very introspective and can leave people feeling a little neurotic and self-obsessed. In the next chapter, I'm going to show you how to shift your focus from the inside to the outside. This was one of the principles that really created a significant change in my thinking and I often bring myself back to it if I'm experiencing too many negative emotions. It's where we find a true sense of purpose and meaning in our work. If we want to be truly fulfilled, we have to find something to contribute to that is bigger than ourselves.

CHAPTER THREE
MAKING YOUR VALUES VALUABLE

> "You can't connect the dots looking forward; you can only connect them looking backwards."
> - Steve Jobs

Up until this point, we've been solely focused on ourselves. It's important to know what you want, but this can only bring you a certain amount of happiness and fulfilment. As cliché as it might sound, true fulfilment only comes when we put the focus on helping someone else.

When I'm working with freelancers and small agencies that have been running their business for ten years or more, they can struggle to find meaning and a purpose in their work. Once they have covered the bills and bought a few nice things, they start to wonder what's next. They ask questions like "how do we take things to the next level?" Or "what's all of this really for?"

It's easy to think that if you just had a few more clients, you could hire more people and take yourself out of the day-to-day running of the business. Although it's a great goal to strive for, it's not going to reignite your passion and make you want to jump out of bed in the morning. In fact, anytime someone is trying to take themselves away from their business, it's a sign that they aren't clear on their values, vision and mission.

A lot of people have this dream of retiring so they can sit on a beach and sip pina coladas every day. The thought might sound appealing, but the reality is somewhat different. Although I didn't have enough money in the bank to retire, I certainly spent plenty of time sitting on beaches and drinking cocktails, whilst maintaining an income from my business. It's fun at first and it feels great because you're living a lifestyle that is very different to most, but the novelty soon wears off and it isn't long before a sense of emptiness and boredom starts to creep in. Once we have met our own personal needs, we need to look for something that is bigger than ourselves.

I realised this once I started to study some of the most prolific entrepreneurs in history. The one thing most of them have in common is that they are still working, despite the fact they don't need to. Richard Branson, Bill Gates, Warren Buffet, Tony Robbins, the list goes on. I remember having a heated discussion with my uncle at a family lunch one Sunday, when I was sharing my new found enthusiasm for these altruistic entrepreneurs. He was adamant that they were greedy and just wanted more money. It's easy to see why people might think this, as they see them living extravagant lifestyles and appearing on the front of glossy magazines. But when I dug down into the stories behind the media portrayal, it became clear that they are all driven by a sense of purpose, bigger than themselves. Think about it, they never have to work another day in their life, yet they still do, so why is that? They have enough money to buy anything they want, travel anywhere and retire, but they keep running their business.

There's a famous saying that if you do a job you love, you never work a day in your life. I believe that is true to an extent, but being passionate and in love with what you do is only half of the equation. The problem with passion is that it wanes over time and rarely withstands the inevitable barrage of challenges we will face on the journey to expressing ourselves through creative work. Purpose trumps passion any day of the week. We need a sense of purpose in our work. We need to feel like what we are doing matters and that our life has some meaning. I know it's easier just to focus on the logistics of running a business and not get existential about the whole thing, but if you can find a higher purpose, it will transform how you feel and give you energy that you've never experienced before. This chapter is about doing exactly that; uncovering your unique qualities and finding a problem to solve in the world that lights you up and is about more than just the skills you've learnt or the lifestyle you want to create.

As we saw earlier in the book, the Japanese have a word for this; ikigai, which roughly translates to 'reason for being'. When I first read about the concept of purpose, I was a little sceptical as I didn't want to find myself in some religious cult. That was, until I came across the work of Victor Frankl, an Austrian psychiatrist who survived the holocaust and then wrote a book about it. Frankl was imprisoned in several concentration camps throughout World War II, including the infamous Auschwitz. His worldwide best-selling book, *Man's Search for Meaning*, describes the harrowing experiences he faced, as well as a theory of why he survived. This theory was later transformed into a style of therapy, known as Logotherapy (it has nothing to do with branding). It's a therapy focused on helping people to find purpose and meaning in their lives. Frankl has hundreds of cases where he has used the therapy to help his patients overcome everything, from depression and anxiety, to substance abuse.

I have witnessed the power of this phenomenon in my own life. Although I didn't discover it through therapy, finding a sense of purpose and striving to create something bigger than myself was the thing that really changed my life and business. I believe that focusing solely on our own desires and ambitions is one of the reasons so many people face mental health challenges today. My intention is to show you how to shift that focus outside of yourself and onto something bigger and more meaningful.

I have read lots of books that discuss the importance of finding purpose and meaning in your life, but very few were practical enough for me to implement. I often felt like I was going round in circles and found myself fluctuating between content nihilism and existential dread. This all changed one day, when I picked up a book titled, *Become a Key Person of Influence*, by Daniel Priestley. At the time, I was in the habit of reading as many books as I could, in the hope that I would find some answers and a reason to not give up. This book was clearly far less philosophical and I didn't expect to find anything life-changing, but when I started reading, I was pleasantly surprised. In fact, the reason you are reading this book is largely due to that moment. It was powerful because it encouraged me to look at my own experiences in life and find a way to relate them to other people. In other words, how might the experiences you've encountered along your journey be valuable to someone else? All of a sudden, my anxiety and unhappiness started to feel lighter and I felt focused and driven.

One of the concepts that resonated with me the most in the book was the analogy that we are all standing on a mountain of value, but often we can't see it because we are too close. We are too busy focusing on what we want out of life, rather than what we can give. I'm not just talking about charity, I'm talking about a unique ability to be of value to someone else, a sense of purpose that is bigger than money or fame or material possessions. You might be thinking that I'm about to try and get you to drink the Kool Aid, but it's far from it. I'm not going to tell you *what* to believe in, just that you must **believe in something.** You must find something bigger than yourself if you want true fulfilment.

One of the conclusions I drew after reading Daniel's book was that I was in a unique position to solve a problem for someone. No one else has the exact same experiences and insights that I have. Nor do they have the same network of people, or the same way of looking at things. No one else is exactly the same as me, and no one else is exactly the same as you. Your ability to solve a problem for someone isn't just about how good you are at your craft, it's about everything that's happened to you in your life, up until this point. All of the experiences you've had made you who you are today. Your unique insights, the people you know, the places you've been to. No one else has that exact combination, it truly is unique. You might think your life isn't that interesting or that you don't have many insights to share, but I've worked with hundreds of creative business owners and I've yet to find someone who doesn't have more value than they realise.

The question is, how do we uncover this value and how is it relevant to our business? How do we make our values align with other people's, and perhaps more importantly, still earn a living doing it? What I'm about to share with you contains the key ingredients for doing exactly that. It's a bit like putting together a jigsaw puzzle; first you have to get all of the pieces out onto the table and then you start to sort them into sections. You might start by looking for the edges or all of the pieces that are part of the ground or sky. As you build up the picture, it all begins to come together and it's easier to find the pieces that fit.

As Steve Jobs famously said, it's about connecting the dots and finding the hidden themes in your life that have always been there. It's about pulling out the lessons from those experiences, good and bad. These things may not seem relevant to your business at this point, but if you can join the dots, it will allow you to see things in a whole new light. It will allow you to tap into your true potential and create a bigger impact with your work.

There is a huge amount of value locked away inside your story and most people look straight past it. We can get so focused on our skills and qualifications that we forget to look at the things that really make us different from our competitors.

When I'm coaching my clients, I use the analogy of an iceberg. Above the surface are your skills, qualifications and portfolio. This is what most people shout about and show off to the world. Although it's important, it's not where your real value is found. It's not what makes you different from everyone else. In fact, from a client's perspective, it's difficult to distinguish between you and another freelancer with a similar portfolio. What tends to happen is your work gets judged purely on price, speed and quality. As you know, there is much more to that than choosing the right person for the job. If you really want to differentiate yourself from the competition, you have to look at what is buried underneath the iceberg.

Under The Iceberg

Being at the top of your field in your chosen craft will get you so far, but there comes a time when you reach a ceiling. A time when you become comparable to other people in your field also at the top of their game and it becomes difficult to stand out. When that happens, most people focus on improving their skills, refining their style or buying more expensive equipment, but this will only create very incremental gains. Instead, you need to look at the things that make you unique, I refer to this as 'looking underneath the iceberg'.

I'm going to share a process with you that I use with my clients to help them stand out from the competition without learning new skills, buying expensive equipment or refining their style. It will help you to see that everything you need to break through that ceiling and become more valuable is already in front of you.

When I first went through this process, I struggled to see how my hobbies and interests related to my work. I felt like I was clutching at straws to make things sound relevant. But as I focused on interests and hobbies that didn't currently earn me money directly, I started to realise how everything was related. For example, I have been interested in personal development and psychology for over a decade. I've read hundreds of books on the subject and invested thousands of pounds to work with some of the world's leading coaches and mentors.

When I first started my coaching qualification, I attended several taster days to see which one would be the best fit. It quickly became apparent that I had already been using a lot of the tools and strategies that were being taught and applying them to my own life. I saw how my own experiences had given me insights that other people in the room didn't have. The more I paid attention to these themes and experiences, the more they became relevant. I started to see that no single skill alone was going to get me to where I wanted to be, and it was about more than building websites for people, taking photos or helping them with their digital marketing. It wasn't about getting more qualifications or adding bigger clients to my portfolio, it was about uncovering the value I already had right in front of me. The combination of experiences, insights, network connections and hobbies that put me in a unique position to solve a problem for someone. The bigger that problem was, the more impact I could have and the more money I could earn. It suddenly dawned on me that my real value was locked away inside my story, the one thing that was unique.

Although my clients' work is incredible, it's not the thing I admire the most about them. What inspires me is the story of how they got to where they are today. The challenges they've faced, the places they've travelled to, the subjects they geek out on. That's what is really inspiring. One of the exercises I do with my clients to help them see the value of their story, is called the 'river of life'. We start with a huge sheet of paper and draw a winding river. The top of the curves represents the high moments in life and the bottom represent the low moments. As we go through, we look at the events and people that have made them who they are today, the themes that are recurring and their defining moments. As my clients go through this process, they start to see the value that they had previously been missing. The things that were right in front of them that never seemed relevant or interesting.

I'm always shocked at how many people have never told their story to anyone because they don't think it's interesting. When they see other peoples' reaction to their story, they realise how much of an impact it can have. It reminds me of when I studied media and film at A level and we had to deconstruct and criticise several scenes of well-known films. We watched the same few scenes over and over again until we knew exactly what was coming next. By the time we had finished, I never wanted to see that film again. Yet for someone who had never watched it before, it was really exciting. Your story is the same; because you have seen the making of it and know it inside out, it doesn't seem that relevant or exciting, but from the outside, it has a completely different meaning.

It's important to realise that there is intrinsic value in your story and it's actually the hidden gem you've been looking for. It gives you a perspective on the world that no one else has and it puts you in a position to solve a specific problem for someone. Your skills are just the tool, but your story and everything else under the iceberg are the things that really allow you to add value.

The other great thing about your story is that it helps you to decide what to focus on. Clients often tell me how competitive their industry is and how it's hard to stand out in a crowded market. When I take time to learn more about their business, I usually find they are generalists, offering a wide range of services and trying to appeal to everyone. It's very difficult to stand out from the competition when you are trying to serve lots of different people, rather than focusing on just one industry or sector.

When I was freelancing, I tried to be as broad as possible because I believed it would increase my chances of winning work. I thought that the more I could offer, the more people I could help. After years of people telling me they didn't really understand what I did, I finally decided I needed to be more specific about who I worked with. The more specific you can be with what you do and who you help, the easier it is to stand out from the competition. Most clients want specialists, not generalists. They may say they want someone who can do lots of things, but what this usually means is they want several problems solved but can only afford to pay one person to solve them.

In business, when you focus and specialise, it's often referred to as having a niche. It's essentially a gap in the market where there is an opportunity to solve a problem better than it's currently being solved. There are great examples of companies who have created powerful niches all around us.

Think of brands like Uber, Airbnb and Netflix. The founders were able to spot an opportunity and look at the problem differently because of the things that exist under the iceberg; their experiences, their network and their insights. The good news is, you have exactly the same ability and it will help you to stand out from the competition and have more impact with your work.

As creatives, there are several reasons we want to avoid niching. Some I've mentioned above, but the one that strikes fear into most people is the idea of doing the same thing day in, day out. We love variety and hate it when life is monotonous and mundane. It's the main reason I spent years trying every creative profession under the sun and refused to focus on one. At one point in my journey, I was running a record label, a digital marketing consultancy, a photography business and producing music, all at the same time. I was craving variety, but it just led me to being burnt out and ineffective. I had too many plates and no matter how hard I tried, I couldn't spin them all at the same time. I was so afraid of focusing on one thing that I did the complete opposite. The crazy thing is that when I went about finding a niche in the right way, I had the best of both worlds!

In my coaching business, no day is ever the same. I might be coaching clients, recording podcasts, designing content, taking photos for my website, the list goes on. Yet I'm very clear about who I help and exactly how I help them. I know you might be saying, "that's ok for you, but I'm a graphic designer, not a coach". I hear you and you wouldn't be the first person to say that. What I'm going to show you in the coming chapters, is that you are more than your craft. Just because you are skilled at graphic design, doesn't mean you have to define everything you do by it. So how do we uncover that value and find the things in our life that are relevant to our business?

Finding Your Niche

By unpacking your story and uncovering your niche, it allows you to find a sense of purpose and meaning in your work. If done well, it will be clear to your dream clients why you're the best person to help them solve the problem they have. The best way to think of a niche is in terms of who you would love to help and what problem they have that you can help solve.

One of my mentors helped me to unpack my story and uncover a clear niche that was in front of me the whole time. He started by asking me to go back to my early childhood and think about what subjects or activities I was often drawn to. He then asked me to notice which of these themes stayed consistent throughout my life. For example, I used to love making things and being creative as a child (which most of us do), but as I got older, that never really went away. Despite going to a traditional school where creativity and art wasn't high up on the academic agenda, I managed to find an outlet and pursue creative subjects. It was clear that creativity was a continuous theme in my story. I had always been passionate about photography and filmmaking, and as soon as I left school, I jumped at the opportunity to work for my cousin's film company in New Zealand. Those themes have never really left my life and I carry a camera almost everywhere I go.

So you might be thinking, what this has to do with my coaching business. Well, when I'm coaching photographers I really understand the nuances of photography, so I can enter their world and fully understand their challenges, which improves the results they can achieve. But really, it's about more than that, it's about the creative process, it's about the passion we have for our craft and the challenges of dealing with clients that don't always share that passion or see the value in the years of experience you have. I've been there, I get it.

To uncover all of these themes and find our real value we first need to pour all of the pieces out onto the table and then sift through to find the parts that we are actually going to use. When you are going back through your story, you will probably start to remember things that seem irrelevant to your business, but it's important not to discount anything at this stage. For instance, I loved magic when I was growing up and I always wanted to perform for people. I wasn't quite sure how this was relevant, but once I had gone through this process several times, I realised the thing I loved was seeing people's reactions and changing how they felt. Making them believe that maybe, just maybe, it really was magic. This is now a theme in my life because a big part of my coaching is about changing people's emotional states and giving them "aha" moments.

As I mentioned in the first chapter, life is less about the vehicles we choose (magic or performance) and more about the emotion are trying to achieve (making a difference or feeling significant). There are lots of ways you can change someone's emotional state or make them think differently, but it became clear to me that coaching was the most logical vehicle for me at this stage. I had been immersed in the world of personal development since my early 20's and continually found myself geeking out on it, so it just made sense to use all of that knowledge and experience.

Take five minutes to go back through your life and look at the themes that keep coming up. Were you always fascinated with health and fitness, for example? What did you spend your evenings and weekends doing while you were at school? These themes are the key to uncovering your niche and tapping into your unique value. Take a trip down memory lane and look at some of your experiences objectively to see what you can gather. It's easy to skip these exercises, but I promise you, this is well worth spending some time on and could be one of the most valuable exercises you do.

My top five themes are:

1:

2:

3:

4:

5:

Now you have some ideas of themes, we need to look at where they intersect. Before we do that, let me give you an example of a client I worked with, called Scott, who had a huge amount of value right in front of him that he wasn't using.

When I first met Scott, he was in a similar position to a lot of creative freelancers and small agencies. He was doing work he didn't really want to be doing. This was regularly showing up in his life as a lack of passion and direction. Clients were continually beating him down on price and he really struggled to communicate his value and differentiate himself from other designers. As a result, he was taking anything that came his way, often being underpaid and undervalued. Scott thought that if he continued to build his portfolio and work with bigger, better brands, eventually his dream clients would come knocking at his door. I completely understand that thinking and it's what I built my entire marketing efforts around when I first launched my business. As we've now seen, this is a big mistake that many people make.

The problem was Scott wasn't clear on who he really wanted to help and who he could add a significant amount of value for. He was putting himself out to the world as a graphic designer that had a varied portfolio of work. This might seem great on paper, but to a client, there is no difference between Scott and the designer on Fiverr. When we started to unpack Scott's story and look at all of the things he had done in his life, there were some clear themes. For example, Scott regularly climbed and had been on expeditions to some of the world's most remote locations. He lived and breathed outdoor brands and when he wasn't designing, he was doing something related to these two categories. To Scott, graphic design was what he did to earn money and everything else was separate. From the outside, it was clear that he had a huge amount of value to offer in these areas and was in a unique position to help a very specific type of client.

By going through this process, we changed Scott from a graphic designer to someone who is passionate about helping outdoor and adventure brands to bring their ideas to life through visually engaging content. All of a sudden, he had a focus and knew where to look for new clients. Not only that, but he was already surrounded by these people, so he could easily start conversations with them to find out their goals and challenges.

To be clear, I'm not saying that you have to turn all of the things you are passionate about into a job. In fact, this can often have the opposite effect and make people fall out of love with the things they are passionate about. Instead, we need to look for the themes in those areas of your life. If you are passionate about yoga and have a keen interest in nutrition and diet, the theme could simply be health and wellbeing. If you are a woman, it could be women's health and wellbeing. The key is to identify the overarching themes rather than getting bogged down with the specifics. If my clients are struggling with this exercise, I often ask them what they geek out on. What I mean specifically is; what can't you stop reading up on, watching videos on and talking to your friends about when you aren't working?

Once you find this sweet spot, you start to see how you really are in a unique position to solve a problem for someone and add value to their life and business. It gives you a clear sense of direction and a reason to get out of bed in the morning. It gives you compelling answers to the questions: why do you do what you do? Why does this all matter, and why should anyone care?

The answer to these should be something that you can go on a rant about. Something that gets you fired up and that you can't help but talk passionately about. For example, when I answer those questions it sounds something like this:

I help talented, ambitious business owners working in the creative industry to unlock their true potential, so they can do meaningful, fulfilling work. Work that makes them come alive, that lights up their soul and creates a positive impact in the world. I believe creativity is the thing that makes us unique as humans. My mission is to empower people to use this creativity to make the world a better place. We don't need more people doing bread-and-butter work to pay the bills. We need people who are passionate about solving real problems, bigger than themselves. We only have a short time on this beautiful planet, so let's make it count.

Defining Your Why

When you decide what your business is really about, your life will change forever. I know that's a bold statement, but something happens when we find a calling bigger than just your craft. I'm fairly sure that is why religion has been around for thousands of years and will continue to influence the world for thousands to come.

It's important to point out that your why doesn't have to be something that changes the course of history. It doesn't have to be the abolition of slavery or changing women's rights, it can be something small and simple. Sometimes for my clients, it's as simple as doing something that makes their environment less polluted and a nicer, healthier place to live. In fact, it's usually better to start small and grow your vision with your business. It's about what is going on in your world and the things you care about.

So, how do you find this big why and where do you start? The good news is, it's already there, we don't have to reinvent the wheel. Your why is up to you, there is no wrong or right answer. Your why can usually be found at the intersection of your themes. It's based on a problem you are passionate about solving and a group of people who would most benefit from having this problem solved. Let's go back to the example of Scott. If we just look at the intersection between design, outdoors and adventure, it was clear that he wanted to help businesses and brands operating in this space to amplify their reach. This would allow more people to have incredible experiences, like Scott, enhancing the quality of their life.

If you find it hard to think about things that inspire you, then think about what annoys you. What really pisses you off? What could you rant about until the cows come home? What gets you excited?

By now, hopefully you are ready to get out into the world and make a bigger impact with your work. The question you should now be asking yourself is: how do I make money from this? It's great having things that get you fired up, but how do you turn that from a charity into a business?

First, we have to get really clear on exactly what the problem is and who would benefit the most from having it solved. We then need to work out if these people are willing to pay us to solve it. second and most importantly, they have to be people we would love to work with and can go to and start a meaningful conversation. These are your dream clients and the next section is about getting clear on exactly who they are and how to find them.

CHAPTER FOUR
FINDING YOUR DREAM CLIENTS

> "I love being a graphic designer, but could we get rid of clients somehow please?"
> - Erik Spiekermann

For a lot of freelancers and small business owners, there's an idealistic world where we can all just create great art and get paid handsomely. The problem is, the idea is based on the assumption that clients are a pain in the ass, and they are only there to pay the bills. When you run your own business, it's usually your responsibility to go out and find work, but when you have looming bills and a shortage of projects on the horizon, it's easy to start panicking and take on anything that comes your way.

Although this solution might work in the short term, it can be a vicious cycle. You take on projects that you wouldn't usually entertain, just to make ends meet. These projects take up a lot of your time and cause a lot of stress. You end up resenting them and they drag on for much longer than you anticipated. This cycle repeats itself until you become burnt out, jaded and resentful of the people you are doing the work for. Over time, I've seen this cycle destroy the passion of some very talented creative practitioners. When our craft feels like work, most people want to give up and start questioning why they are even doing it in the first place.

Imagine what your life and business would be like if you loved everyone you worked with, they paid you well, and you saw the amazing results they achieved from working with you. How might things be different? Speaking from personal experience as well as from years of industry experience, I can assure you this is possible. However, there are a few common mistakes that people make when choosing who they work with.

The first is being way too broad. Trying to be everything to everyone is the fastest route to being overwhelmed, burned out and lacking passion. Not only that, but it just confuses people and reduces the value of your work. It seems counterintuitive being so specific about who we want to work with, as logically, it would make sense that the broader we are, the more chance we have of getting work. The problem is that's only from our perspective. Put yourself in a client's shoes for a second and ask yourself who you would rather work with; someone who specialises in solving the problems they have, or someone who works with everyone and anyone?

It's not just about the client's perception either, it helps you in so many ways when it comes to attracting the type of work that you really want to be doing. Imagine you're at a networking event and someone asks what you do, if you say you are a graphic designer, how likely are they to remember you? Even if they do, they probably know lots of graphic designers. You may get lucky every now and again, but it's definitely not a sure-fire way to get referrals from people that don't already know, like and trust you.

However, when you are specific about who you help, what challenges they have and how you help them, people are much more comfortable recommending you. It feels like they are recommending an expert, rather than a random graphic designer they met at a networking event. It eliminates a lot of the risk on behalf of the person recommending you because they know you understand the problem and if you share your story, they feel like you are the perfect person to help solve it.

I did an experiment using LinkedIn a few months ago where I connected with people in the creative industries and offered to introduce them to a potential client. I asked everyone I connected with who they wanted to be introduced to and I was quite shocked with the response. Out of hundreds of people, there were only about five or ten who gave me a detailed description of who they would love me to introduce them to. Everyone else had responses that could roughly be translated to "anyone". The problem is, I don't know where this mysterious anyone is hanging out, they seem to be so hard to pin down! Unfortunately, I wasn't able to introduce any of those people to anyone in my network. However, the people who told me exactly who they wanted to be introduced to got several introductions.

Once we have an idea of the sector we want to focus on, we need to go a level deeper and get really clear on the type of person we want to help. In the world of marketing and business, this is often referred to as a customer avatar. It's a detailed description of a person that represents your dream client. This is the best way I know of getting really clear on who you want to work with and winning projects that are both creatively fulfilling and financially rewarding. In this chapter, I'm going to show you how to create one and avoid some of the common mistakes people make.

Be Aspirational

The one thing that surprises me the most about working in the creative industries is the amount of people who tolerate bad clients. Whether this is because we tell ourselves we need the money or is driven by the reward of having a particular brand on our portfolio, it seems to be a common theme.

It's unlikely that we would tolerate these kinds of people in our personal life, so why do we convince ourselves that it's ok to tolerate them in our business? When we get clear exactly who we want to work with, we also need to get clear on exactly who we don't want to work with. This will help us to filter out the bad eggs and leave us with a roster of clients we are proud of. In order to do this, we must be aspirational with our standards. What I mean, more specifically, is aiming beyond what we may believe we can currently obtain.

I once heard someone say that you should shoot for the stars because if you miss, you can always land on the moon. As strange as that metaphor might sound, it's very translatable when working with your dream clients. If you aim for average, the best you can get is average and below. However, if you aim for aspirational, you could get them, and below that will be taken up by good and great clients. Leave no room for bad clients in your business (however you define them).

Over the past few years, I've become fascinated with peoples' standards; in other words, what people will or will not tolerate. I've learned that people with low standards for relationships are usually driven by a sense of fear and scarcity, whereas people with high standards in a relationship are driven by a sense of abundance. This relates to all areas of life, whether it's a romantic relationship or a business relationship. We only tolerate bad clients because we believe in some way that there aren't better options available to us, so we settle.

Hopefully, by now you've started to realise that you have so much more to offer than your skill set. You are more than enough, and your dream clients and projects are available to you, you just need to know where to look. In the next chapter, I'm going to be sharing a strategy with you that will help banish any form of scarcity that you might have. Before we do that, we need to get really clear on exactly who we want to work with.

If you get specific and commit to raising your standards, you will have a freelance business that is truly rewarding and a base of clients you love working with. I can honestly say that I love every single one of my clients and it makes a huge difference to how I feel about my business, day-to-day. If I start working with someone and they violate the boundaries we have agreed, or they start to do something that goes against my values, I immediately give them their money back and stop working with them. I have no reason to work with people who I don't like or who I'm not going to get a great result with. I operate from a place of abundance, knowing there are thousands, if not millions, of people in the world who I can really help and who I would love to work with.

Now you have a clear idea of your core values, you can use these as a guide to determine who to work with and who to avoid. We are now going to take it a step further and get really clear on the attributes of your dream clients and why you want to work with them. This means sitting down and thinking about who you would really love to work with. Who would you crack open the champagne for? Most freelancers are afraid to do this because they think that by aiming for aspirational clients, they will put off the good and average clients. In my experience, the opposite is true. You attract better clients because they too are aspirational.

For example, over the last few years, I've worked out that my aspirational clients are established freelancers or small agencies that have been running their business for over 10 years. They have likely won some awards and have some prestigious clients on their portfolio. I aim for these types of clients all of the time. I talk to them in my marketing, I ask for referrals from people I know. Although I'm lucky enough to have a large number of these clients, I still get a high volume of people who don't meet this criteria applying to work with me. So why is that? It's because people are aspirational.

When I first started working with one of my mentors, he clearly stated that he only worked with six-figure business owners who wanted to scale to seven-figures. I didn't have a six-figure business, but I still got in touch with him because I *wanted* a six-figure business and knew he could help me. I aspired to be like the clients he worked with and that was the important thing. Before we get into too much detail about our customer avatar, we need a quick sense- check on three key criteria. These are the three basic criteria that your dream clients must meet, in order for you to be able to build a successful freelance business.

1: You love working with them and they allow you to live your values.

This is really important because if you don't enjoy working with them and don't really care about their business, your work will eventually start to reflect this. As professional as you are, consciously or subconsciously, this message will start to shine through. One of the reasons we identified our values early on is because we now have a reference point when it comes to new clients or projects. We can stop focusing on specifics and ask ourselves if this client or project will allow us to live our values on a daily basis. Is this work going to give you the feeling of freedom, respect and significance you truly desire? If the answer is no, **do not** take on the project. Make sure you run through the values exercise properly to ensure you have plenty of ways to get these values met.

There is a common belief that nightmare clients are just part of running a business, but I have plenty of case studies to show that this isn't true. If you have a large base of clients you don't like or that you find it difficult to work with, it says a lot about your standards, as well as your process. The law of averages says that you will get 1-2 nightmare clients per year, but it's your choice how you deal with those clients and how quickly you get rid of them.

2: You must be able to add significant value.

Most people just deliver whatever is asked of them, and don't stop to assess the amount of value their product or service is having on a client's business. For example, when I used to design and build websites, I would charge the same price to a small independent business as I would to a larger corporation (if the project was a similar size). I soon realised that one website was having a significantly larger impact for the client than the other. I did the work because it paid me and I didn't mind it, but was I really creating significant value for that company?

We will talk more about value-based pricing later in the book, but for now, I just want you to become aware of the potential value you are delivering for your clients. Is it creating a transformation for them or is it just a nice-to-have?

We want to look for the clients we can add the most value for and solve a significant problem. This is hugely important because without this, you quickly become a nice to have rather than an essential part of running the business. I will show you how to make your services more valuable in the coming chapters, but for now, just be aware that the amount of money you can charge is directly related to how much value you can add. Having said that, we still need to make sure our clients have a budget.

3: They must be able to afford you.

Affordability is probably an issue you have come across before. The difficulty is that it's often an excuse the client uses when they can't see the clear value in what you are offering. I've had people say they can't afford to work with me and then I see them book a two-week holiday to the Caribbean. What they really mean is that it's not a priority for them to spend that money with me right now. In most cases, price is only an objection in the absence of value. However, we don't want to make life unnecessarily hard for ourselves. If we choose a market where the majority of businesses count every penny they spend, it's going to feel like a constant battle. It's not impossible however and I've got plenty of clients who make good money working in the charity and not for profit sector. Just consider the way the business works and where their available cash flow is likely to be before you get too set on working with them. For example, if you are pitching to a small cafe that has a high number of staff and low-priced food, they are unlikely to spend £3,000 on a rebrand.

Pricing is a big topic, so I'm going to address it separately in chapter seven. For now, just know that some businesses really are in a position where they can't afford your services. Make your life easier and search for the people who meet all of the above criteria, instead of just one or two.

So now that you have three main categories to cross-reference, you need to start contacting those clients, right? The question is, where do you start? I often hear my clients say that they don't know how to find and connect with their dream clients, which is completely understandable, as most of us aren't sales and marketing experts. Before we start thinking about what platforms to use and what to say, we need to get clear on exactly who they are. Once we have more detail about this, it will be so much easier to find and connect with them.

It's a bit like a TV crime series where they are trying to solve a complex murder case. They have a big board up on the wall with all of the images and evidence related to the case and the more pieces they add, the clearer it starts to become as to who the murderer might be. If you don't have clear attributes and details about your clients, it's very difficult to find them. Should we be looking online or offline? Will they be more likely to respond to an email or a phone call? None of these questions can be answered accurately without a detailed customer avatar. When you are thinking about who they might be, I want you to look at the intersection of the themes you identified in chapter two. The key is to have dream clients that you have things in common with, so you can start meaningful conversations.

It's helpful to break our dream client avatar down into three main categories, to keep it simple. I usually label these categories demographics, psychology and location. I start with demographics, as it's easier to build the other two categories from that.

Demographics

Start with the basics like age, gender and nationality. It might be tempting to try and be broad here, as you may have a few different avatars in mind, but for the purpose of this exercise, be as specific as possible. Here is an example of mine:

Age: 38 Gender: Male

Nationality: British Marital status: Married Children? Yes

Annual income: £55,000

These are designed to be the fundamental building blocks of our avatar. You may want to add things that you feel are relevant, which I've not included, or you may want to leave things out. The idea is that we could put this search criteria into a computer and it would be able to return some results.

Location

We want to think in terms of online and offline for this section. Maybe you get a lot of your clients online, through places like Upwork or Freelancer. In which case, you would make a note of that, but we also want to think about how they are spending their time and attention. This is going to be really valuable when we come to actually engaging with our dream clients and getting their attention. It's helpful to think about a specific geographical location. This could be your hometown, or a major city where you know there is a high density of these people or businesses. Where do they spend most of their time when they aren't online?

Psychology

If we really want to connect with our dream clients in a meaningful way, we need to find out how they think. The more you can understand about your client's world, the easier it is going to be for you to get their attention. You need to be able to demonstrate that you understand the challenges they are facing and how what you offer relates to their goals and ambitions. Without this, it's like you're trying to speak to someone in English, when they only speak Japanese. Communication is going to be limited and it's going to be harder to build trust and rapport. When I'm thinking about the psychology of my clients, I want to look at people's belief systems and values. What is really important to them and what do they value about the world? If I can understand this, I have a high chance of being able to help them and clearly demonstrate value.

To start with, you could think about their beliefs about their business and their role within it. Do they believe it's a difficult industry? Maybe they feel it's boring and no one really understands it. What do they think about themselves? Are they confident and outgoing, or do they consider themselves an introvert? I would forgive you for wondering how you would ever know this without meeting them, but for now, I just want you to make it up. We need to start with assumptions, and then we can clarify and question those assumptions when we go out to talk with them in real life. I will give you some ideas of questions to ask your prospective clients in the next chapter, but for now, base your assumptions on previous clients you've worked with and clients you would love to work with in the future.

The last part of the dream client avatar is what I call the 'red rope' criteria. Our values are a great guide to determine who we should and shouldn't work with, but we also need to think about the specific attributes that our ideal client would need, in order for us to create a remarkable result for them. You may say that you want to work with a big-name brand, but what are the attributes of the brands that make you want to work with them? If we find ourselves getting too caught up in the idea of the brand or project, rather than the attributes of the people we want to work with, it's a sign we are off track. Describe them, are they resilient? Open minded? Funny or playful?

When I got clear on the attributes of my dream clients, it helped me with two things; first it allowed me to work with people I actually enjoyed spending time with, and secondly, it allowed me to create better results with them. It's a qualifying criteria that will allow you to filter out clients that aren't a good fit. I know this might sound like it's reducing your chances of finding more work, but like niching, it's actually increasing your chances.

The Red Rope

Imagine you go to a nightclub and you've got VIP tickets, but when you get there you find they are just letting anyone into the section you've paid for. How would that make you feel? The red rope isn't about ego, it's about creating an experience for your clients that gives them the best possible experience of working with you. It's to ensure you are going to have a great working relationship and you can confidently deliver the result you have promised.

For example, my clients have to be ambitious, determined and honest. If they aren't, I can't get a good result with them. If they give up after the first month of us working together, it just won't work. They also need to be good at what they do, or to put it another way, they need a strong, commercially viable portfolio. I have a whole list of criteria that I share with people who are interested in working with me. This way, we ensure that no one's time is wasted and they are going to get what they pay for.

So what attributes are important for your ideal clients to have, in order for you to be able to help them? Maybe they have to be open to new ideas in order for you to get the result they want? Do they have to be resilient and try lots of things? The clearer you are about the attributes of your ideal client, the easier it will be to deliver a great result for them.

As soon as I started being strict with my criteria, it changed how I felt about my business completely. It's a wonderful feeling to love working with your clients and actually look forward to catching up with them, but more importantly, to know you're going to create tangible results. If they don't have the right criteria, this becomes much more difficult.

Think Big, Start Small

You might be left thinking, this is all great, but how am I going to start a conversation with my aspirational clients? In business terms, this is called a route to market and it's very important. It's great having directors of FTSE 100 companies as your aspirational clients, but if you don't know any of them, it's going to be much more difficult to start a conversation.

The key here is to think big, but start small. Go back to your attributes list and think about who you already know that meets that criteria. Do you know a director of a smaller company who you could easily have a conversation with? Who do you know in your network that could introduce you to someone who meets your criteria for your aspirational client?

One of the reasons I love LinkedIn is because it allows you to do exactly that. You can see 2nd and 3rd degree connections and think about who could make that perfect introduction. My clients are always surprised by the amount of people they are already connected to that know someone they want to have a conversation with.

If you have found the intersection between your themes from chapter two, starting conversations should be much easier. What you will realise is that you already spend time with these people or know a lot about them. They are people just like you, who have experienced similar challenges, but aren't quite as far along the journey. In the next chapter, I'm going to share some tangible strategies for communicating your hidden value to your dream clients, so that you can develop long-term relationships and do more of the work you love.

CHAPTER FIVE
ACTIVE VS PASSIVE

> "To do the work you love, you must win the work you love."
> - Daniel Priestley

What if I told you that your dream clients aren't going to come knocking at your door? Even if you spend years honing your craft, polishing your portfolio and tinkering with your website. Sure, you may get enquiries and some of those projects may be fun and well- paid, but it's not a strategy that will fill your diary with high-value clients on a continual basis.

If you are good at what you do, it's likely that you are busy. The question is, are you busy with the type of work you *really* want to be doing? Is it the work that lights up your soul, pays you handsomely and gives you a real sense of fulfilment? If you've got this far, I'm guessing the answer is no.

Whenever someone tells me about the lack of fulfilling or exciting work, it usually comes down to one simple concept; they are being passive, rather than active. What I mean by this is that they are relying on word of mouth, recruitment agencies or direct enquiries for most of their work. This feels like a good option because you don't have to put in too much effort, but it's out of your control. It's also really hard to break the cycle because people usually refer similar clients and determine the price before you've even had a conversation with them. It's easy to tell yourself that you are too busy to go out and look for new work, but the reality is, it's the only thing that will change the calibre of clients you have.

I started my career working for a global marketing and advertising agency. They had every major brand you could think of in their portfolio. I was shocked to find out that, in spite of being one of the world's leading agencies with over 30 years' experience and having created award-winning, worldwide campaigns, they still had to pitch for new business. In fact, they would spend thousands of pounds on a pitch, even if they had no guarantee of winning it!

The world's top agencies still have to actively seek their work, so why would it be any different for a freelancer or small business? I understand that it's not always comfortable and it's easier to sit back and take whatever work comes your way. I also understand that you are busy and maybe don't know where to start, so I'm going to share a strategy with you that has helped my clients win work they never thought was possible.

Before I do, let's look at some reasons why most freelancers and small agencies hate the thought of putting themselves out there, and struggle to be active, rather than passive.

1: You don't know where to start.

One of the questions that my clients ask when we start working on their pitch is "where do I start?". The whole process can seem quite overwhelming and confusing if we don't have some structure and planning. Many people have actually tried pitching to their dream clients and not had much success, so they decide it doesn't work. The good news is that now you are clear on exactly who you want to work with, it's much easier to know where to start these conversations. Just look at where your dream clients are spending their time. The even better news is that these are often places and platforms that you are already using.

2: You don't know what to say.

No one likes to feel salesy, but unfortunately, when most people pitch themselves, that's exactly how they sound. It feels odd offering something to someone you have never met, so we tend to avoid it at all costs or overdo it and sound like a used car salesman. Changing how you communicate with your dream clients is one of the most valuable things you can do. I'm going to show you exactly how to do that later in this chapter, but for now I want you to stop thinking about selling and start thinking about listening. Most of the time, we want to tell someone what we do because we think they might need it. However, as you will see later in the chapter, the most valuable prospects are the ones who don't actually know what they need.

3: It feels uncomfortable.

I used to hate the idea of pitching myself and my business. I was in a business accelerator program run by NatWest a few years ago and we had to stand up in front of a room full of people and give a sixty second pitch, almost every week. Repetition and continual exposure are supposed to reduce fear and anxiety, but even after a few months, it still felt scary. It's natural to feel anxious and uncomfortable when putting yourself out there. No one enjoys being rejected or judged, but unfortunately, it's a necessary part of the process. In the rest of this chapter, I'm going to show you how to overcome these three challenges and even feel good about pitching to your dream clients on a regular basis!

Meaningful Conversations

If you want to feel good about pitching, the first thing you need to do is shift the focus from yourself to the person you are talking to. I often see people posting about their services on social media and then wondering why they don't get much response. The reason is usually because there is no one immediately looking for that service. We are so used to talking about ourselves and what we offer, that we forget about our dream client and what they want. Most people who are thinking, "I really need some new headshots", are the ones who have already started searching for a photographer. It might seem illogical, but you are much better off not talking to those people. To explain why, we need to look at the process most people go through when they are considering making a high value purchase. Think about something you have bought in the last few years that was a considered purchase. In other words, you didn't just go out and buy it spontaneously. Look at the diagram below and see if you can identify with this thought process.

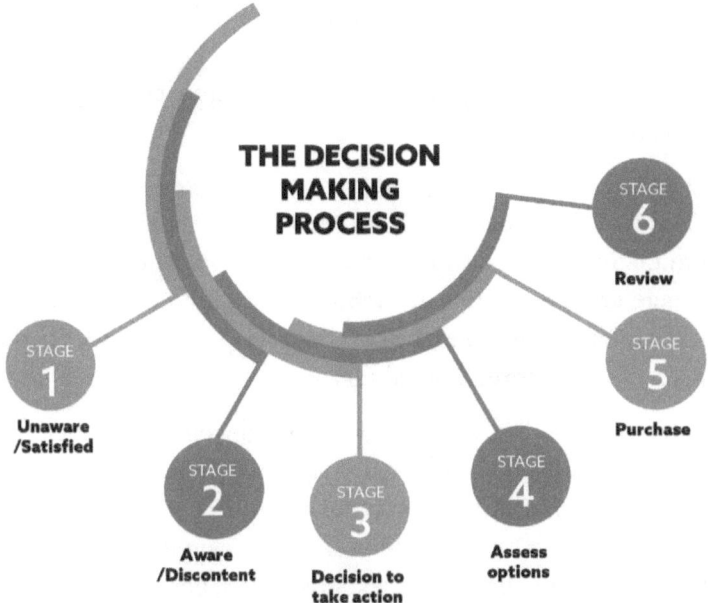

You probably started at stage one. This stage is where you aren't even aware you have a problem or are happy with the current solution. Let's take a new piece of equipment as an example, maybe it was a computer or a camera. You were happy with it, but then maybe something stopped working or a new model came out on the market. All of a sudden, you moved to stage two and are now aware that the solution isn't quite as good as it was. Maybe the new model has features that would make your workflow easier or give you a better-quality image.

There is a tipping point between stage two and three, which lasts longer for some people than others. Most of us have something in our life at this moment in time where we are between stage two and three. We are aware there is a problem, but we haven't yet decided to do anything about it. When we get tipped over the edge, we move to stage three, and then quickly to stage four. We go out into the market and research possible solutions in an attempt to find the best solution. Once we have found the best option, we then make a purchase (stage five) and review that purchase (stage six), to check it was the right decision.

The interesting thing about this process is that most freelancers and small business owners are pitching to their dream clients at stage four of the process. Prospective clients at this stage are already out in the market looking for a solution to their problem. This seems like a logical place to talk to them, until you look at three critical factors.

The first is that only 20-30% of the entire market are at stage four, ready to buy. That means you are missing a huge section of the market you can engage with. The second factor is that stage four is where everyone else is vying for attention, which means it's hard and expensive to get it. Think about getting to the top of Google or running paid ads to people who are using specific search terms. It's going to be the most competitive and therefore expensive place to advertise. The third and final factor is the criteria that people are using to assess options at stage four. In most cases, people are looking at quality, price and speed. They want the thing that is the best quality, for the best price, in the shortest time possible. This creates a race to the bottom, and you end up competing in a noisy, competitive marketplace on all three of those factors. So, what's the alternative?

Start At The Beginning

What about, instead of engaging with your dream clients at stage four, you start a meaningful conversation with them at stage one or two? A conversation that is about them and what's happening in their world, rather than you and your services. Wouldn't that be easier and feel more comfortable?

If we are going to engage with people at stage one or two, we need to change what we are saying, as well as who we are saying it to. The reason I'm asking you to start as many conversations as possible is so that you really understand your dream clients' challenges and goals, not just guessing. What are they thinking? What keeps them up at night? What frustrates them on a daily basis? The more we can understand their world, the easier it will be to engage with them, build trust and demonstrate value.

I want you to start thinking of yourself as a detective, your job is to find out as much information about your dream clients as possible, so that you can really help them. For now, forget about exactly how you are going to do that. Many people struggle with this at first because they have such a strong identity attached to their skills and constantly think of every problem in relation to them. For example, if you are a graphic designer, you immediately start thinking of how you can help people with graphic design. As we've seen from chapter two, that's not always a good thing.

When I ran my freelance business, I was so busy promoting my services that I forgot to listen to what my clients wanted and ask the right questions. Because I didn't understand what was going on in their world, I attracted people who thought they knew exactly what they needed, how much they were willing to pay and how quickly they needed it. It put me in a position where I felt like a creative monkey for their ideas, being ordered around constantly, changing colours, resizing images and being blamed when things didn't work.

It's far more powerful to help someone who knows they have a challenge, but doesn't know exactly how to solve it, than it is to help someone who already knows exactly what they need. The reason being that you can demonstrate value and position yourself as the expert or the guide, rather than the donkey carrying the bags up the mountain! One of the most powerful things I learnt from one of my mentors was that when you can explain someone's problems better than they can, you earn their permission to solve them.

CHAPTER SIX
STARTING MEANINGFUL CONVERSATIONS

> "Let us make a special effort to stop communicating with each other, so we can have some conversation." - Mark Twain

The more conversations we have with our dream clients, the easier it becomes to really understand what is going on in their world. What you realise is that when you get specific about who you want to help, patterns appear in these conversations. The same kind of challenges and goals will crop up over and over again, which will then inform your future interactions. After a few hundred conversations, it will seem as if you already know what they are going to say before you have even met them. I've had people tell me that they felt like I have known them for years, even though I had only spent a few hours talking to them.

Starting meaningful conversations doesn't have to just be online, networking events are also a great place to do this. The key is to make sure you are asking the right questions and interacting with people in a way that puts them at the centre of the conversation. It's important to keep the concept of meaningful conversations at the forefront of your mind. In my experience, to have a meaningful conversation, there are three things that must happen:

First, we must be present and not be constantly engaging with our internal voice that is worrying about how we look, or what people think of us. I know that's easier said than done, but it's actually a skill you were born with. Remember a time in the past when you were completely engrossed in a conversation, maybe it was with a close friend or family member. One of those conversations where time just seemed to fly by, and all of a sudden, you had forgotten to have dinner or pick your nan up from the airport. You weren't engaged in your internal voice; you were just focused on what that person was saying and listening intently.

The second thing is to remove the agenda. Go into a conversation without the intention of getting something from it. Just to be clear, this isn't the same as not having a variety of ways you can help that person, if the opportunity arises. I'm simply suggesting that you don't have a fixed outcome in mind. This way, we will find out if we can genuinely help them or if we may be able to introduce them to someone else who can.

The third part is to be curious. What I mean by that is to refrain from judging what the person is sharing. It's almost impossible to be empathetic with someone if you are judging them. Again, this comes down to disengaging from our internal voice, but being curious and letting our intuition guide some of our questions.

To help me remember this, I use the acronym P.A.C - Present, (no) Agenda, Curious. When I'm in business-related situations, I keep this at the forefront of my mind. It might help to imagine something related to that word, for example, you could think about how you are creating a pact with someone or you could imagine a giant PAC man eating power pellets. Whichever one works for you.

This is such a simple concept, but it can really transform the results you get in your business. It will also help you transform how you feel about approaching new clients. As soon as you make it about you, all of the fear, doubt and insecurity creeps in, but as soon as you can focus on the other person and open a space to have a meaningful conversation, all of that disappears.

This works really well when we are having a conversation with our dream client, but what about when we are talking to other people. If you've ever struggled to answer the question, "what do you do?", then the next section will be really important for you to understand and master.

The Power Is In The Pitch

As creatives, we don't want to pigeonhole ourselves because there is so much we can offer beyond our skill. The problem is that if we are too vague or broad, people don't remember us, and it doesn't help us to attract our dream clients. If we just pitch ourselves based on our skills, then we are going to attract people at stage four of the decision-making process; clients who already know what they want and are comparing on speed, price and quality. So what we want to do is create a pitch that attracts our ideal clients at stage one and two of the process.

To do this, we have to take everything we are learning from our conversations and put it into a simple formula of who, what, how and why. When this formula is crafted well, it can be the difference between people queuing up to have a conversation with you and struggling to get anyone's attention. Let's take a look at those four things separately and help you to create this statement for yourself.

By now, you should have a good idea of who you want to work with, so the first part is to put them in the equation. That usually looks something like; I help (dream client). The second part (what) is about the outcome or challenge you help them to overcome. The third part is about how you do it, and then finally, why that is important. For example, my clients usually find it helpful to say something like "I believe" or "I care strongly about" when talking about their why. We have spoken about all of these things already, but if you ask the right questions when you are speaking with your dream clients, this will become much easier. I will be giving you some specific questions to ask in the next chapter, but at this point, use these statements as a guide.

Let's look at some examples: my client, Scott, went from saying he was a graphic designer, to saying, "I help outdoor and adventure brands to bring their ideas to life through visually engaging content." Scott can then explain all day about why he believes that is important. Another client, Will, is passionate about the environment and sustainability and he now helps ethical and sustainable brands who want to make an impact but struggle to stand out from the competition. Racheal works exclusively with non-profits and charity organisations to help them raise awareness, increase visibility and communicate the impact of their work.

I could give you countless examples of people that have a clear pitch and therefore find it much easier to start conversations. When you are clear about who you help, how you help them and why you care, it leaves people feeling clear, confident and excited. Referrals and introductions become much easier because people have something specific to go on.

When you get this right, it can be transformational for your business because it is clear and concise yet focuses on the challenges and outcomes so we don't get pigeonholed. There is one problem with having a clear statement like this when it comes to pitching for new work though. I don't know if you've ever been added by someone on LinkedIn with one of those kinds of titles? In most cases, I ignore them, because I just feel like they are going to try to sell something to me.

If you've ever sent out cold emails or used LinkedIn to prospect for new business, but had little or no response, then you were probably presenting yourself in a similar way. We want to be continually reaching out to people and starting conversations, but we don't want to be salesy and put people off before they've even had a chance to talk with us. So how do we go about doing that?

When I first started my coaching business, I had very few relevant contacts, no reputation and no online presence. Therefore, I had to be really active, constantly reaching out to potential partners and starting meaningful conversations with my dream clients. To this day, I still reach out to people and pitch on a regular basis, just like those big agencies. The difference is, I'm not pitching for business. Never in my life have I emailed someone asking if they want coaching. Mainly for the reasons I've discussed above, but also because I don't know enough about that person to be confident I can definitely help them. Instead, I pitch what I call a 'high-value, low risk offer'.

Don't Propose On The First Date

When you don't already have an existing relationship with someone, you need to find a way to build trust and demonstrate value before asking for anything in return. You may have heard of a book called *The Chimp Paradox* by Professor Steve Peters. In the book, Peters talks about the primal part of our brain that he refers to as the 'chimp'. The chimp is always looking for danger and keeps us on high alert for anything or anyone that can harm us or steal from us. It's the sceptical part of our brain that thinks of anyone outside of our network as a stranger. Whenever I'm reaching out to someone new, I always think about pitching to the chimp. I want to get the chimp on my side before I even try to talk to the human.

So going back to the question of what to say to our dream clients, I've found there are four key elements that need to be included in any communication, to get the chimp on your side. The first is a reason for contacting them. Don't ask me to explain the science behind it, but research has shown that people are more likely to agree to a request if you give them a reason (the chimp works in mysterious ways). The second thing we need to include is a genuine compliment. The chimp loves to be made to feel important and respected, no matter how rich and famous they are. The third is a relational anchor, in other words, something that shows you are on the same team. The best relational anchors are mutual connections, but if you don't know any of the same people, think of something that you share an interest in. This just creates some common ground and helps the chimp to feel a bit safer.

The final, and most important, part is to offer something of value. This is the where we want to reduce the risk as much as possible. You may not think that meeting for a coffee is very risky, but for someone who is busy and values their time, there needs to be a clear benefit for them. Think of something you can offer that would give them some tangible value and wouldn't take up lots of their time and energy. If you approach your dream clients with them and their chimp at the forefront of your mind, it will change how you feel about pitching. But more importantly, it will change the outcome you get from your pitch.

Let's say you've been starting lots of conversations and you begin to get some replies, what now? Finding and attracting your dream clients is a little bit like dating, if you appear eager and too keen on the first date, you are probably going to scare them away. I'm sure you've been around someone in the past who makes you feel uncomfortable because they are clingy and come across a little bit desperate. Your dream clients will sense this energy and either take advantage of you and try to get lots of things for free, or not engage with you any further.

This is another reason why it's important to have lots of conversations simultaneously, it ensures you aren't hanging all of your hopes on one client. Staying with the dating analogy, if you are dating lots of people at the same time, you are in an abundance mindset. In other words, you feel like there is lots of opportunity around you. If you are only dating one person every few months, you start to move into a scarcity mindset, feeling like this is your only chance to find a partner.

When you start approaching your interactions this way, you will find that people get excited about the prospect of you helping them and want to find out more about your services. However, you still want to take things slowly and, instead of jumping in with a proposal, spend some more time building that relationship.

Have you ever had a meeting with a prospective client where it seems to be a perfect fit? They need exactly what you can offer, they have the budget and you end the meeting talking enthusiastically about how you are going to work together? You spend a few hours putting a proposal together and send it across, but hear nothing but crickets. This would happen to me a lot when I first started my freelance business and, for a long time, I couldn't work out why.

Eventually, I realised that I was jumping the gun and that I hadn't taken enough time to build trust and demonstrate value. I was usually asking for a sizable investment and the project could take anywhere between six months and a year. That's a big commitment for someone who doesn't really know you and has just heard about you through a friend. It's a little bit like going on a date with someone your friend has set you up with and then proposing to them straight after. In order to demonstrate that you actually understand the challenge they have and propose a solution that is relevant, you have to take them on a journey.

Think about the strongest relationships in your life, they are usually with people you have shared significant experiences with. You can take this observation and apply it to working with your dream clients. If you create an experience for them, it will allow you to build trust and demonstrate value. If you pay attention, you will notice that all of the world's best brands do this. They let you experience the product, before you actually own it. Whether that is being able to use a MacBook before you buy it, test drive a car or look around a house. Most of the big purchases we make, we get to try before we buy. So what would our business be like if we offered this to our potential clients? In other words, showing them you can help by actually helping them.

The Logical Next Step

A logical next step is a process in the overall journey that makes it easy for the prospect to experience what it is like working with you, without having to invest a significant amount of time and money.

Every good business is trying to reduce risk and increase return on investment. Therefore, we need to play to that. You have to realise that in the past 20 years, the barriers to entry have lowered significantly, meaning anyone can start a freelance business with just a laptop. Clients are becoming increasingly cautious and have usually been stung in the past by a project that went wrong. So why should they trust you? It's great having a referral, but even then, it's not always enough to make it a done deal.

When your clients are dictating what should be done on a project, what they are really trying to do is ensure they have control and reduce the risk of things going wrong. Ultimately, this means they don't trust you or the process, for whatever reason. In order to demonstrate that we know what we are doing and that the process works, we need to create a logical next step.

A logical next step has two main criteria; firstly, it must demonstrate value, and secondly, it must involve a relatively low investment of time and money from both parties. It's no good if you're just going out and doing work for free because then they won't value the rest of what you do. You need to find a way to demonstrate value in a short period of time. The way to do this is through clarity and insight. That means showing clients the real problem, creating lightbulb moments and providing them with a clear path to a solution. The question is, how do you create clarity and insight for your potential client, without investing a significant amount of time and energy for free?

This is where you need to get creative. I can give you some examples of what my clients have done in the past, but what's right for them might not be right for you. Your logical next step needs to demonstrate value, and often, people use this as an opportunity for a diagnostic or strategy session. A lot of people (myself included) are worried about giving all of their ideas away because they think the potential client will just go off and steal them. What I've come to learn in recent years is that ideas are essentially worthless, as a great idea without any implementation is just an idea. If people want to steal ideas, then let them. If those clients want to go to the effort of implementing them, then wish them luck and make a note to check in with them in a few months time. It's likely they will have to experience the challenges of a DIY solution before realising they need your help. The key here is not to be aggressive or negative towards their decision in any way. Continue being helpful and providing them with anything they need. For example, I often send people a book on the topic which I've found useful. These people may never become clients, but I can assure you they will talk highly of you to other people and it will increase your reputation ten-fold.

Another concern people have is that the potential client will just use someone cheaper. Again, I say good luck to them. There is probably a reason that person is cheaper and it's unlikely they will really get the end result they are trying to achieve. However, if they can get that result at a lower price by going to someone else, that's when you need to look at how you can add more value and create an even bigger transformation.

One of my favourite examples of a logical next step was created by a client of mine, Steve, who was a stonemason.

When he established that his ideal client was an architect, the question then became, how can he demonstrate value to architects in a short space of time? Steve told me this great story about walking around his local town and just walking into architects' offices covered in dust and debris. He certainly got people's attention and simply asked if they took on any public art projects. He made the conversation about them and their challenges rather than himself. Obviously, the conversation got around to him very quickly as people were curious about his appearance.

Steve arranged to have meetings with these architects to dig further and find out more about their challenges and goals. He found that they had a common challenge which was that whenever they applied for public art projects, they often got stuck at the planning stage. As Steve had a fair bit of experience with these, he put together a short guide that outlined everything they needed to help them win these types of projects.

He then went back and shared the guide with them for free. They found it hugely valuable as it saved them a lot of time and showed them how to generate extra revenue. Guess who they asked to be involved in creating sculptures when they won a project?

You want to ensure your potential client values what you are offering. If it is free, there is a chance they won't, but if it's too expensive you fall into the trap of proposing on the first date. Do some research on the industry and find out how much they would be likely to spend to overcome these sort of challenges. If you can't find this out, the best way is to ask people. You will be surprised how many people tell you if you just ask them.

Another way to get around this is to ask for a donation to a charity or make it clear that you are waiving the fee for a limited time. For example I offer a strategy session that helps people to get clarity and insight around their key challenges. They leave with a much better idea of what to focus on in their business and have a strategy to follow in order to achieve their goals. Based on feedback, most people find these calls valuable and I've sold them in the past for around £150. I give people the option to book a call through my website for that amount, but I also offer a limited number for free. This way, people value the call much more than if I just offered them for free all of the time.

Just remember, whatever you decide to offer as your logical next step, it must meet three criteria: it gives people clarity and insight around their challenges, it is perceived as valuable and it doesn't require a significant investment of money and time. Once your prospective clients have taken this step, they should be in a position where they can see the road ahead much more clearly and have had some valuable lightbulb moments. Once you have a tool or strategy that can create this predictably and consistently, you will find that you start to attract a much higher quality client. The key is to track these interactions so that you can see what part of the process needs to be improved.

C.A.M.P.S

As I mentioned earlier, the main reason anyone experiences an inconsistent income and the dreaded cycle of feast and famine is because they aren't constantly having meaningful conversations with the right people. This might seem obvious, but most people realise it too late. They only realise they haven't had enough conversations when they don't make enough sales. The problem is, it's too late to do anything about it by then. That's why you need to measure conversations, not sales.

Your aim should be to take your prospective clients on a journey where you can demonstrate value and build trust. In order to do that, you need to have a process to follow. Seeing as I have an acronym for most things, I thought I would create one for this! C.A.M.P.S is a reminder to measure four important metrics; Conversations, Appointments, Meetings, Proposals and Sales.

A conversation is any time you talk to someone who may have a problem or challenge you can help them overcome. This means if you send out 50 messages and 20 people reply, you've had 20 conversations. If you go to a networking event and have five meaningful conversations, that counts too. Conversations are a powerful way to get real insights into your dream clients' challenges and add real value. I was only able to write this book and design courses that transform my client's businesses because I had hundreds of meaningful conversations. Without those, I would've just been guessing what people were struggling with and how to help them.

Once you are comfortable with starting meaningful conversations, you can move to the next phase, which is arranging an appointment to discuss challenges and goals they have for their life and business in more detail. An appointment is an agreed date and time that is in both of your diaries. Saying, 'great, I will give you a call' or 'drop you an email next week', isn't enough. You are still in conversation mode. We want to take this from a conversation to a meeting.

It's the right time to offer an appointment when you have uncovered a challenge or goal in the conversation that you can potentially help with. The idea of booking an appointment is to discuss these challenges in more depth, demonstrate value and then propose to help, if appropriate. There needs to be some form of qualification here, so if you are unsure, go back to your red rope criteria.

So what's the difference between an appointment and a meeting? Well one is agreed, and one is an actuality. Just assume that at least 10% of your appointments won't ever turn into meetings. People are polite, so they agree upfront, but things happen at the last minute and priorities change - that's just life. It has nothing to do with you or your business. However, we still need to measure the two separately because if you book 20 appointments in a month, but only 10 people show up, we know something is causing the prospect to have a perception of that meeting that it isn't valuable enough to them. If we don't measure this, we can't see where the chain is breaking.

Finally, if you have structured the meeting correctly, it's likely you will uncover a need or a goal that you can help the prospect to overcome. This is when you create a proposal to move forward with your logical next step.

It's important to remember that there will be a delay to your activity and sometimes it can feel like you are doing everything right, but nothing is happening. This is when it's most important to continue the process. By neglecting your prospecting activity this month, you will notice the impact in the next 2-3 months. I talk to my clients about the 30-day rule, which basically says, what you do in the next 30 days will bear fruit in the next three months. This rule is almost like clockwork. I was coaching a client recently who had reached out and started a conversation with someone they had dreamt about working with for a while. They were happy they got a response, but felt nothing really came from the interaction. Then suddenly, seemingly out of the blue, they got in touch and commissioned my client for some work. My client never imagined they would be able to work with such a prestigious client with just a string of well written emails, let alone in the space of a few short months. By being consistent and adding value, they were pleasantly surprised.

Be warned though, if you stop reaching out and having conversations whenever you get busy with other projects, it will have an impact a few months down the line and that's why consistency is key. In the next chapter, I'm going to show you how to take your dream clients through the decision-making process, in a way that is elegant and leaves them feeling valued.

CHAPTER SEVEN
HOW TO SELL WITHOUT FEELING SALESY

> "Selling is something we do for our clients - not to our clients."
> - Zig Ziglar

Over the past few years, the one thing that has had the most impact on my life and business is learning how to have a structured sales conversation. When I decided that I wanted to build a more meaningful, impactful business, I started to study and work with people who were doing just that. From the outside, it looked like they were just passionate about their business and had a drive and hunger that surpassed others. When I dug a bit deeper, I realised they weren't just passionate about what they did, they were world-class salespeople. Working with various mentors and reading hundreds of books has made me realise that if I want to have a bigger impact, I have to learn how to become much better at selling.

The problem was, I had a negative association with sales. I thought It was boring, cheesy and out right manipulative at its worst. I had a belief that it was only done by people who weren't good at their craft or had a bad product, so they had to find other ways of convincing people to buy from them. Since then, I've come to learn that every world-class business has world-class salespeople.

We all have different ideas of what sales means; some of us imagine men in suits sitting in fancy restaurants. Others think of call centres or automated voices asking if we have recently been in an accident. Whatever image we have, most of them are fairly negative. The truth is, none of us like to be sold to, but we do like to buy. If we ever feel like we are being "salesy", we stop immediately and run 100 miles. When I ask who loves sales during my talks and workshops, less than 5% of the room usually raise their hand. So what's going on?

Sales, like anything, is a skill that can be learnt. Like all skills, it can either be learnt well, or learnt badly. There are lots of people who learn the wrong way to sell, and very often, they are the ones who leave negative impressions in our mind. Most of the time, when someone is good at selling, we don't even feel like we are being sold to. That's the key distinction here. The reason you hate sales is because your experience of sales is about being sold to, not buying. You love buying, in fact, there is a lot of pleasure associated with buying for most people, to the extent where it is nothing short of an epidemic.

Having had the privilege of being mentored by world-class entrepreneurs who are also incredible at selling, I've learned the difference between good sales and bad sales. There is a way to have a sales conversation that feels good for both people, even if they never become a client. This chapter is all about helping you to do exactly that, but before I get into the strategies and principles of good sales, we need to spend some time reframing what sales means. As I mentioned at the beginning of the book, I can give you all of the best strategies that can make you thousands of pounds and give you a huge amount of fulfilment, but if you have negative associations, you won't use them.

Reframing Sales

The truth is that most freelancers working in the creative industries aren't getting paid what they want because they don't know how to sell what they are offering. You might be thinking, well, I've been earning money up until now, so I must know how to sell a bit. I would argue that you know how to take a brief someone gives you and work to it. That's not sales. In fact, it's actually the opposite of sales. You can do more damage by taking on work that isn't a good fit for you or the client. If you believe that by saying yes, you aren't being salesy, and anytime you try to convince someone of something you are being pushy or salesy, then you are going to struggle.

Most of our negative emotions around sales are created by focusing too much on ourselves and having a belief that the conversation is about trying to convince someone of something and prove ourselves in some way. If you have done the steps in the previous chapters, this is easy to reverse. When you engage with the right people at the right time, everything feels so much more natural and it seems that people are actually selling themselves.

There is a saying that "telling isn't selling", which basically means 80% of the conversation should be the customer talking and 20% should be the salesperson talking.

When I started to learn about the sales process from my mentors, I saw that selling wasn't about me at all; it was about the person I was having a conversation with. Instead of being in my head and worrying what they thought of me, I just listened to the prospective client and asked intuitive questions, without a hidden agenda. When I really listened, I came up with questions that no one else had ever asked them because they were too busy trying to sell them something.

This opened up a whole new world for me and sales actually started to feel good. I left each interaction with a sense that I had really made a difference to that person and their business, even if they never became a client. People can sense that intention and your conversations will feel completely different. Better still, most of the people who never became clients, ended up recommending me to people who did.

The only way you are ever going to change your mind about sales is when you realise what your current beliefs are costing you. Have you ever seen someone be commissioned for some work and thought, how have they got that? My portfolio is way better than theirs!? Have you ever seen the person or company that got the job you were bidding for and wondered what they did differently? Unless they already knew the client and were on good terms with them, the likelihood is that they were just better at selling themselves than you were.

If you are really going to break through the glass ceiling and take your freelance business to the next level, you must master sales. The good news is, 'sales' in my dictionary, probably isn't the same as in yours. So first, we have to be committed to changing our beliefs around sales and implementing what you learn here, not just using it as theory. The first thing to acknowledge is that most people struggle with sales because they have no structure to their conversations. My clients often tell me they don't know what to say or feel, as though the conversation is just meandering from side to side, without really going anywhere. They are afraid they are wasting the other person's time or are hiding their true agenda.

In this chapter, I'm going to give you a framework that is used by some of the top sales professionals in the world, to create powerful conversations with prospective clients. Conversations that leave them feeling like they have received value and had an enjoyable experience, even if they don't sign up to work with them. Not only that, but the sales conversation actually determines the tone of the whole relationship moving forwards. It's where you create boundaries and agreements for working. It's where you demonstrate that you are the expert and the guide.

Before we move forward, I want you to just check in and notice what you feel when you think about sales in general. Is it positive or negative? Do you get excited or bored? Take a few minutes to answer the following questions. Do not proceed until you feel excited about learning how to have a powerful sales conversation.

What are my current beliefs about sales?

Are any of these beliefs stopping me from taking action and having more sales conversations?

What impact are these beliefs currently having on my business?

What does this impact look like when it is magnified 5 to 10 years into the future?

Would these beliefs have an impact on any other areas of my life?

If I had the opposite of this belief, what sort of action would I be taking today?

If this belief were true, how would I feel about sales?

What Do They Really Want?

When I first started learning about sales, I had a major lightbulb moment that transformed the way I communicated to potential clients. I was working through a Tony Robbins program where he kept repeating the idea that people buy based on emotion, and then they justify it with logic. Up until this point, I had been talking to people about the features of what I was offering, which created very little emotion. The question I asked myself was "how could I get people to become emotional about a website or graphic design?"

What I came to realise was that it had nothing to do with the website or graphic design. That was just the vehicle. Like I mentioned in chapter one, we don't want the vehicle, we want the value. Your potential clients don't want the website, they want what they think the website will give them. I eventually realised that it wasn't about the product I was selling; it was about the emotion they wanted to feel. Now all I had to do was work out what that emotion was and ensure what I was offering was going to give them that.

Think about a big purchase you made within the last few years. Maybe it was a holiday, or a new car. You might have been thinking about the holiday or the car when you made the purchase, but there would have been a feeling attached to it. Don't get me wrong, this isn't easy to do, but it is something you can learn. In order to create emotion for people, we have to work out what the cost of **not** taking action is, and what the reward of **taking action** is, in emotional terms.

I'm going to show you how to do this without being deceptive or disingenuous. This isn't about creating something for the sake of selling to someone. It's about helping people to see what is below the surface of these wants and desires. Just like you have done for yourself by identifying your values, you now have the opportunity to help someone else. Emotion really is the driving force behind all human behaviour, and if you can understand what is driving someone, you can help to guide them. You don't have to be a psychologist to work this stuff out, you probably do it naturally. I'm just going to give you a framework and some questions that will ensure you do it in a way that isn't forced or unnatural.

The Two Islands

I want you to imagine there are two islands, Island A and island B. Island A is where your prospect is now, and island B is where they want to get to. Your job is to work out what both of those islands look like and what is stopping them from reaching their destination. If they have already worked this out, then the conversation becomes a lot less valuable (unless their assumptions are wrong). This is why it's so important to engage people at stage one or two of the decision- making process, before they have figured out the whole plan for themselves.

Let's use the example of a website. If a prospect was at stage four of the process, they might come to you with a list of things they want their new website to have. However, if the prospect comes to you at stage one or two, they are going to be describing how they want things to be, rather than what is going to get them there. Using the metaphor of the two islands, it's a bit like someone asking you to build a boat versus someone asking you the best way to get across the sea. The second person is going to get much more value from you helping them and see you as the expert. The first person is going to see you as a boat builder. That's why it's so important to dig for the goal behind the goal. What do they really want? What will that ultimately give them? Sometimes they may not even have a clear picture of island B, but what most people can do is use their imagination, especially if you help them.

One of the ways I get my clients to describe this is by asking them what it would look like in an ideal world. Our dream clients might not know exactly what they need, but they know what they want, we just have to help them to describe it.

Now we have a good idea of what island B looks like, we need to make sure we also understand exactly where they are now. What is the lay of the land? When you are talking about island A (where they are now), you will want to make sure you get really clear on everything you need to know, in order to make an accurate diagnosis. Going back to the idea of the detective, imagine all of the things that would influence their ability to make it across the water. You may ask if they already have a website or how they currently promote their business. I'm sure you already do this to an extent, but if you break the conversation down into sections, it gives it much more structure.

The final part is talking about the gap between the two islands and exactly what you need to do to cross it. Before you start diagnosing problems and making suggestions, you need to make sure you both have a clear picture of the two islands and what is standing between them. If they don't know there are shark infested waters, then they won't put any value on avoiding them. Let's talk about the value of showing them the gap.

Mind The Gap

There is a famous proverb that is often used to emphasise the importance of understanding the potential consequences of seemingly insignificant things. It goes like this:

For want of a nail, the shoe was lost. For want of a shoe, the horse was lost. For want of a horse, the rider was lost.

For want of a rider, the message was lost. For want of a message, the battle was lost. For want of a battle, the kingdom was lost. And all for the want of a nail.

It is a great way to remind yourself that until the client sees the full extent of the gap between island A and island B, they won't put much value on it. Imagine it's a sunny day and they can see the other island, it looks like a short swim and you tell them that it's going to cost them ten thousand pounds for you to help them get there. How likely are they to pay you? However, if they knew that there was a pot of treasure on the other side and that the waters were infested with sharks, do you think they might value that offer differently? It's the same with sales and getting your prospective clients to see the value in what you are offering. If it just looks like a logo to them, they are going to compare it to Fiverr. It's your job to explain that branding is much more than a logo and what happens if they get it wrong. A lot of freelancers and small business owners don't want to do this part, they just want their clients to understand the value already. The problem is, if the client has already worked out the value for themselves, they will be at stage four of the decision- making process. As we now know, that is where people assess options based on time, price and speed.

So how do we get them to see the size of the gap? The secret is in asking the right questions. Remember the phrase "selling isn't telling?" Well, what we don't want to do is just tell them that there are lots of sharks in the water. We have to ask them questions that allow them to see the sharks for themselves.

We want them to understand the cost of not taking action or choosing the wrong option. We want them to understand that crossing the gap isn't easy and requires years of skill and experience, the kind you have.

I encourage you to think of a few questions you could ask your dream client to help them see the size of the gap. I will share a few of mine with you, but what works for me, won't necessarily work for you. It needs to feel natural and genuine. The questions are best asked once you have identified a challenge, for example, lack of sales or customer engagement.

Once I identify a challenge, I want to know why that challenge is significant. I will ask questions such as, "what impact has that had on your life or business?" and "what would it look like in three years' time if things stayed the same?" I'm not just doing this to make things seem worse than they are, I'm working out if I'm the right person to help them bridge the gap between the two islands AND if it's going to be valuable for me to do so.

Becoming The Guide

Once you have worked out what island A and Island B look like and you both agree on the size of the gap, you can ask if they would like some help crossing it. If the answer is yes, now is the time to play the guide.

Your dream client will want to know as much about the process as possible. What is involved, how are we going to make the journey, how much will it cost etc. At this stage, I don't want you to hold anything back, in fact, I want you to give away all of your best ideas and strategies for free. When I give this advice to freelancers and small agencies, their first reaction is often a concern that the potential client will steal the ideas and use someone else who is cheaper. As I've said previously in chapter five and six, there will always be people who do this, but it's the only way to position yourselves as a partner rather than a worker. If they want to go and get someone to build them a metaphorical boat and sail it across the ocean themselves, then let them. You will always get these kinds of clients that have to learn the hard way. The question you should be asking yourself is: do you want to be the boat builder with lots of angry people coming back because they almost drowned, or the guide who is busy dealing with clients who respect and value what they offer?

By making the client the hero of the journey and making yourself the guide, you have a valuable relationship that is seen in most narratives throughout history. The relationship you create with your client starts way before you have begun the work, in the sales conversation. This is where you get to determine if they see you as the boat builder (worker) or the guide (partner). The sales conversation is your opportunity to not only serve them and create valuable insights, but to take control of the relationship.

It's not about being dominating and it has nothing to do with ego, it's purely from a practical and safety perspective. Who do you think will be a better guide, the person who has lived on the island most of their life and completed the journey a thousand times, or the person who has done some research and formulated a plan? Just remember, this only works if you spend time unpacking your story and finding the intersection of themes. You have all of the knowledge and experience you need, as long as you are operating within a niche that aligns with your story from chapter two.

Being Ok With Saying No

When I ran my freelance business, I used to have a belief that just because someone asked for my help, I was obliged to give it. Even if I knew the person wasn't a good fit for the product, I would find a way to adjust what I did so that I could help them. Like I said in the previous chapter, I wasn't focused on whether the client was a good fit for what I was offering, I was focused on helping them to work something out because I believed it was my job. You can't help everyone and trying to do so is going to lead to one of two situations: burnout or being broke. In some cases, it leads to both, which is detrimental to business.

Despite my best intentions, I couldn't help everyone. It wasn't possible from a capacity perspective, but more than that, it wasn't what people needed. I was afraid that if I said no, there wouldn't be enough work out there. The reason I had that belief was because I wasn't starting enough meaningful conversations on a regular basis (see chapter five). When I started conversations consistently and was specific about who I wanted to work with, I realised that I had to say no to people that weren't a good fit.

No is one of the most powerful words that you can learn to say. Not only does it give you more authenticity and credibility, but it also makes you feel more confident in what you are offering. When you know exactly who the product is right for, it will give you more certainty in your sales conversations. Ultimately, that is what people are buying, the certainty that you can help them to overcome their challenges and get them the result they want.

In the next chapter I'm going to talk about how you create that result as well as some of the common mistakes that freelancers and small agencies make when trying to create it. Let's look at your most valuable asset: time.

CHAPTER EIGHT
STOP SELLING YOUR TIME

> "Your greatest resource is your time."
> – Brian Tracy

Have you ever had a client come to you because they need your services, but they don't have the budget? In this scenario, there are two options most people choose. The first is to reduce your price, and the second is to reduce the scope of the project. In my experience, both of these are bad options.

Reducing your price gives the impression that you were too expensive in the first place and will lead to the client feeling hard done by if they ever have to pay full price. This isn't the biggest mistake of the two though. Reducing the scope of the project is actually worse than reducing your price. I say this because if you reduce the scope of the project, you aren't really providing a solution to the problem that your client has. Providing you have done the work in the previous chapters, you should now have a clear idea of the problem you are solving for your client. Once you know this, you will then be providing a solution to that problem, but if you reduce the scope of the project, it's no longer the solution, just a part of it.

It's a bit like going to the doctor and being prescribed antibiotics, but not taking the full course and still expecting to be cured. Some clients want to take a few of the antibiotics you have prescribed them, a few from a friend and finish the course with some paracetamol. They try to bodge things together, thinking that they are saving money, but really, they are just making things worse.

This was something I used to let happen far too often and when I look back, it was born from a place of inexperience and fear of losing the client. I would compromise on so many things just to keep them happy. In the end, it never worked out, because they didn't get a solution to their problem. The worst part was that they would never admit any blame because they were relying on me to guide them. Instead of taking control, I took a backseat and just did what they asked. I was a worker rather than a partner and was constantly being compared to other people with the same skill set.

In order to stop this from happening, you need to change what you are offering your clients. Instead of thinking about what they want, start thinking about what they need.

Sell Them What They Want, Give Them What They Need

Once I had learned how to have a structured sales conversation and uncover the real wants and desires, I realised that what I was offering wasn't going to get them there. I needed to do two things: the first was to get clear about what problem I was solving, and the second was to be clear on what I needed to do, to be confident I could actually solve it.

The best way I have found to do this, is to work out the steps in the process that are involved in getting them from Island A to Island B. One of my favourite questions to ask when I'm going through this process is: if I only get paid after I got them from A to B, what would all of the steps be to ensure I received my fee? This question changed how I thought about working with my clients. Instead of just delivering something and hoping it worked, I started to take responsibility for the result. I realised that there were specific steps that must happen if the process was going to work. Letting the client dictate that process was a big mistake. Once I took control and insisted that my clients follow the process, not only was I able to charge more money, but I was creating completely different results. They were much more tangible, and I could start to prove a return on the money they had invested.

It was so effective that I now help my clients to implement this exact same process in their businesses. For example, I work with a video production company based in London and when they first became a client, they had a large price range for their projects. Sometimes they would have small one-off projects for a few hundred pounds, and other times, they would have big projects for thousands. The problem was that they were at capacity and couldn't really take on more work, but had hit a ceiling with their revenue. In our initial strategy session, we identified that they were often allowing their clients to dictate the process. They were cutting back on the scope of the project to meet needs and budgets and allowing them to pick and choose what they wanted from a menu of services.

In one of our coaching sessions, the directors had a challenge with a client who wasn't happy. Knowing that I had experience working with film, they asked my opinion on the work to sense check quality and consistency. It was clear the work was of high standard and followed the brief, but the client still wasn't happy. When I asked them to go back to the client for more detailed feedback, what became clear was that the client hadn't achieved the end result they actually wanted. When I discussed this with the directors, they told me that the client was demanding and had insisted on dictating the whole process and then wasn't happy with the end result. Maybe this has happened to you before? You do everything the client asks, but they still aren't happy. That's because the client isn't the expert, so they shouldn't be in charge! Going back to the metaphor of the two islands, it's a bit like someone sailing the boat who's never really sailed before, capsizing and then blaming the person who built it.

The way to avoid this is to be clear on the process and make sure that you present it to the client in the sales conversation. Once you have positioned yourself as the guide, they will want your advice about how to get from A to B. This is the part where you can show them the best route and walk them through the journey.

At this point, a few people tell me that each project is completely unique and they take someone through a different process each time. When I hear someone say this, it's usually a good indicator that they aren't clear enough about who they help and what problem they solve. If you are at this point, go back to chapter three and get really clear on those two things. Just remember, you aren't stuck helping this person forever. It's just a starting point to give us some focus, ensure you are actually creating tangible results for your clients and begin getting paid what you deserve.

Map Out Your Process

Take five minutes now to map out the steps you would have to go through with your dream client in order to ensure they got the result they wanted. I find it useful to start with the two islands in my mind. Where are they now and where do they want to be? Then think about all of the steps that you would take them through to ensure they got the result.

Below is an example of what the two directors of the video production company came up with:

Step 1: Clarify business objectives and set metrics

Step 2: Define target audience using our persona workshop Step 3: Create video content plan

Step 4: Implement content production Step 5: Measure and improve

What you might notice about the process above is that it isn't going into great detail about each step. For now, I don't want you to get too hung up on the minor details, I just want you to think about the things that would have to happen to ensure you achieve the result and more importantly, to show the client that you achieved it.

Take five minutes to map out your process now.

You may find that when you present this to clients, they tell you they have already got parts of the process or they don't need them. What you must understand is that this is your process and it will be different to how they have done things previously.

If you've ever bought a new car that is under warranty, you know that you can't just go and buy random bits for it and then expect it to still be covered. The car has to contain all of the original parts from the manufacturer for them to guarantee that it will get you from A to B. Your process is no different. You can't just start adding bits in from someone else's process and expect the same outcome. I often use this analogy when I'm faced with this objection, and nine times out of ten, it works.

On the rare occasion it doesn't, I won't take them on as a client and will refer them to someone else.

Now we have our process, we want to bring this all together into a tangible offer that is linked to the end result. I want you to start thinking about this more like a product, rather than a service. Once you see that people don't want your time, they want the outcome, you can create an offer that delivers it.

Building Your Offer

One of the activities I ask all of my clients to do is to take all of the ideas from their head and put them into a brochure. Something that your clients can hold and that you can walk them through with them during a sales conversation.

I've been told several times that this activity alone is worth the time, energy and money that they have invested in my program. The reason being is that it forces you to get really clear on what you are actually offering your clients. They can see it and touch it, which makes it much more real. Having something physical also signifies that you aren't just having a nice chat over a coffee, you are having a sales conversation. In order for the offer to have some substance, there are a few things you will want to include. Firstly, I would suggest you give it a name. This is one of the best ways to make it real in people's minds, and if it's related to the ultimate result they are hoping to achieve, it will make it that much more powerful.

One of my clients is a graphic designer who works with established entrepreneurs who are looking to launch a new business or product into the market. His offer helps them do this and is called the 'unfair advantage'. Another client designs interactive games, and his offer is simply called 'the game creation accelerator'. It doesn't have to be complicated and sometimes you want something that simply does what it says on the tin.

Once you have a name, you can start designing the rest of the brochure. I would encourage you to include a snippet of everything you have discovered so far. Your values, story, the clients you help (who, what, how and why) and the process you take them through. It's also helpful to include some case studies or testimonials. Don't worry if they aren't specifically related to your offer, for most people, this will be brand new. When I first launched my offer, I included testimonials from people who had worked with me in the past. I would even encourage you to make it clear to the client that this offer is brand new and that you want to use them as a case study. You can offer a slight discount, in return for a testimonial and a referral.

Features Vs Benefits

One of the key distinctions to make when presenting our offer to people is the difference between features and benefits. A mistake I see a lot of creative freelancers make is spending far too much time talking about the features of their offer and not getting clear on the benefits to the customer.

Let's use the example of a website. The features might be that it's built on WordPress, has fast load times and is mobile responsive. The benefits of these features are what the customer cares about, not the features themselves. In this example, it might be that you don't have to pay someone every time you want to make a change, meaning you save a huge amount and can spend more money driving traffic and making sales. The benefit of mobile responsive means that people can buy your products from any device, which will result in a higher volume of sales. Always think about what the feature means to the client and why it's important.

I would strongly recommend that you include 3-5 features in your brochure that are unique to your process and way of working. Under each feature, list out the benefit to the client. This way, you can easily reference them in your sales conversation.

Creating A Collective

At this point, you would be forgiven for wondering how you are going to deliver all of this on your own. Most people worry that, as a one man/woman band, they can't help their client to achieve the result they are looking for on their own. Sometimes this is true, and you have to find other people to help. There is a huge trend at the moment where freelancers and micro agencies are coming together to form flexible teams, often referred to as collectives.

It's a bit like making a film, each person would work on that film for a set amount of time and then when it was finished, they would move on to another one. I believe this is the future of freelancing, teams coming together to serve bigger clients, without the overheads of an agency. One of the reasons I regularly bring industry leading creatives together is because I have seen the power of this type of collaboration first-hand. A benefit of my coaching program is that it connects people at similar stages of their journey who they can share these ideas and experiences with. It's not uncommon for my clients to team up and combine their skills. By doing this they are able to create an offer that they wouldn't have been able to deliver on their own.

That being said, you don't *have* to be able to create the ultimate result for the client. It's about linking what you do to provide that ultimate result. They need to be able to see that what you are offering is going to help them to get to where they want to be. Going back to the metaphor of the two islands, maybe what they actually want is to climb to the top of a mountain on island B. If you help them cross the ocean and go from island A to Island B, that's going to get them a lot closer to that goal. You may not be able to help them climb the mountain or introduce them to another guide at that point, but there is still a huge amount of value in helping them get there in the first place. This brings me to the next question I get, which is all around pricing.

How Much Should You Charge?

One of the hottest topics in the world of freelancing is pricing. I hear it constantly from my clients, as well as in forums. How do I know how much I should charge? What should I say when people ask for a discount? The list goes on. I'm not going to get tactical here because the truth is, there is no one-size-fits-all answer.

However, what I am going to do is outline a few universal truths that completely changed the way I think about how to charge for a product or service. It all comes down to this: how much you charge should be in direct relation to how much value you add. So the question then becomes, how do we know how much value we are adding? This is the part that I can't answer for you, but what I can tell you is that the clue lives in the gap between where they are now and where they want to be. The size of the transformation you can create for someone is directly related to the amount of value you can add.

Let me give you an example. Let's say you are building a website for someone. You may assume that all websites are created equal. However, the exact same website for one company will be 10 times more valuable than for another company, all depending on what problem they are trying to solve.

One website might already have lots of traffic and the new font, branding and user experience was what was needed for people to start taking the actions they were looking for. However, the exact same, beautifully designed website, given to a company that has hardly any traffic, won't produce the same results. This may seem like an overly simplified example, but it applies to all creative businesses. There is no one-size-fits-all solution and that's why it's so important to really unpack your value and find your niche (see chapter two). Your ability to add value is tied up in your story, and you have the power to create a much bigger transformation than you realise. You just need to use everything under the iceberg to help solve a problem for your clients.

You may find it easier to think in terms of percentages, rather than money. This was one of the things that allowed me to remove the emotion from pricing. After running my first few courses, I started to build some case studies. I started to measure the things that people had told me they wanted to improve, such as reducing stress, increasing revenue and having more fulfilment in their work. After six months, there was a difference, but the real uplift came after a year. In some cases, my clients had increased their revenue by over 4 times. If you could double your revenue, reduce your stress and find more fulfilling work over the next 12 months, how much money, time and effort would you be willing to invest to make that happen?

Asking your clients these sorts of questions can feel uncomfortable at first, but you have to realise it's for both of your benefit. It's not about how much you think it's worth or what you believe you are personally worth, it's what the client believes it's worth to them. What would it be worth to the person you are creating the transformation for? So what happens if you find out it isn't worth much?

Feedback, Not Failure

I was always scared of presenting new ideas and asking too many questions to my clients in case I found out that my services weren't actually that valuable. It was one of the biggest traps I fell into in the early days of running my freelance business. Instead of getting some really valuable feedback and insight into how I could solve a bigger problem and improving my offer, I just kept doing the same thing. I fell in love with my services, rather than the challenges and goals the client had. As creatives, it's easy to get caught up in this narrative about our personal value or worth. The truth is you don't have an intrinsic value. The market decides what your offer is worth based on the problem you are solving and how many people you are solving it for.

Getting emotionally attached to your ideas leads to feeling like a failure if people don't like it or don't want to pay for it. It's hugely important to separate your personal worth from the value of the product you are putting out into the market. One of the reasons there is so much resistance to putting ideas out there is that people feel as if they are personally being judged. This will cause you to shut off valuable feedback that could help you to improve your offer.

What would your service look like if you asked more questions about what wasn't working and saw every piece of feedback from clients as an opportunity to improve? Would you still be offering the same thing as you are today? For the next few weeks, I want you to go out into the market with your new offer and show it to everyone you know. Ask them what they think of it and if they would buy it. Don't worry if they aren't your dream clients, at this stage, we are just practising listening to feedback. Make a note of everything they say and think about how you could improve or change what you are currently offering. This doesn't just work for new customers, it works for existing clients as well. In fact, it's the best way I know of turning customers into clients.

Customer To Client

The main difference between a customer and a client is that a customer buys once, a client continues to buy. So the question is, how do we create more clients?

In order to keep people coming back, you need to do at least three things:

1: Don't upset them

2: Understand the new set of challenges they now face

3: Offer something that can help to solve those challenges

One of the biggest issues is that people stop investing in the thing that has given them the results in the first place. It sounds counterintuitive, but once they have found a solution to their challenge, it seems like there is no need to continually invest time, money and energy. I used to come across this all of the time when I was building websites for my customers. They would pay me for the work and then just leave the website sitting there, without updating it. A few years later, when it stopped working or enquiries dried up, they would come back and tell me it was broken. It became clear that I needed a strategy to educate my clients on the importance of ongoing maintenance. It's usually much easier to keep a client that you've already created a result for, than to win business from someone you've never met. The question is, how do we keep clients after we have created a transformation for them?

I experienced this over the past few years with my coaching business. After six to twelve months, my clients have usually achieved some remarkable results. Some have doubled their revenue, and others have a newfound sense of confidence and purpose. The mistake my clients make is assuming the work is now done and will continue to produce those results, without any external support. Although I give my clients strategies and frameworks that stand the test of time, I found several clients that started to fall back into old habits as soon as they were left to their own devices. I started thinking about what I could offer that would continue to help them after they had achieved what they initially set out to do. By going through the process I've just shared with you, I developed something I call the Creative Life Inner Circle. It's an exclusive group for existing and previous clients that gives them continued support, without having to invest in the program all over again.

I found that there were new challenges my clients faced, which we hadn't previously addressed. Just like in the first sales conversation, I went through the process of working out where they are now, what the next steps look like and how I could help them achieve it.

It's easy to assume this transition should be automatic, but it's not. The fact that you have delivered that level of transformation often means that people believe they have achieved the result they want and there is nothing left to be done. If you want them to move from customer to client, it's your job to show them the road ahead and ensure they navigate the new challenges they will inevitably face.

You might be thinking about a project or client that keeps coming back to you, as long as you deliver work on time, to a good standard and at a reasonable price. That tactic is fine, and it works for a lot of people, but it doesn't make you a vital part of their business. You might have to really let them down before they consider using someone else, but that assumes someone else doesn't approach them with a more compelling offer.

I've heard countless examples of freelancers and small agencies being fired by one of their biggest clients for, seemingly, no reason. They were doing great work, at a reasonable price and always delivered on time. The problem is, that's no longer enough. You need to create a partnership with your clients that means you are indispensable. You need to position yourself where you can show that you understand so much about the company and help them to solve significant problems that they wouldn't even consider an offer from someone else. As I mentioned previously, this is the difference between a worker and a partner.

Workers are dispensable, there is a world full of them and they will work longer hours than you and produce similar quality work for less money. It's not a level playing field because they can live in a different economy, which means they don't have the same living expenses as you. People can look anywhere in the world for their workforce, so you are competing in a global marketplace.

Now you might be thinking, that's not true for me, my client values the fact that I'm local and they can just call me when they need to. That's true, until someone comes along and gives them a compelling reason to use a remote workforce that solves their problems for less money and handles all of their objections and concerns around communication. Someone who is better at having a structured sales conversation and communicating value.

The point is this; you can't compete with tools. The good news is that we don't need to. If you have ever felt like you don't have creative control with a client and you are just a tool for someone's ideas, then you have been a worker. If on the other hand, you've worked on projects where the client is relying on your experience and expertise to guide it and make it a success, then you have been a partner.

Really this chapter is about a never-ending conversation with your clients ensuring that you are solving problems. If you do this well, you will never be short of work. If you want to work with your dream clients, you must focus on creating partnerships with them. That means shifting your mindset, but it also means communicating this intention from the start. Taking your pitch from; "I'm a graphic designer and I can help you do X, Y and Z for this amount," to, "I am here to be a partner in your business, to help you solve this specific set of problems and we are in this together."

It's a subtle shift in language, but it makes a huge difference to how you are perceived and the value you can add for your clients. This approach will allow you to charge more, gain creative control and have more impact with your work. Once you realise you are in a unique position to solve a problem, you will start thinking like a partner instead of a worker.

CHAPTER NINE
YOU CAN'T DO IT ALONE

> "Great things in business are never done by one person; they're done by a team of people." – Steve Jobs

There is a misconception within the freelance and small business world that you have to do everything on your own. I used to read books that talked about multitasking and wearing lots of different hats. In this chapter, I want to show you an alternative that I use to help my clients focus on their strengths and the things they enjoy doing, so they can have more time, freedom and maintain creative control.

One of my mentors used to tell me that your environment dictates your performance. Up until recently, I didn't really understand what it meant. Since I decided to make a conscious effort to build relationships with people who share my values and are creating some amazing things in the world, that advice has made much more sense. A lot of the people I'm now lucky enough to call friends are also part of my team, yet they don't work for me. They are experts in their field, have written books, done TED talks and are regularly featured in mainstream media. I know I can pick up the phone to get practical advice and emotional support whenever I need it. However, this didn't just happen by chance. The environment I put myself in to meet these types of people was critical. I didn't just bump into them down the local pub, I met them at events and on courses that I paid good money to attend.

One of the reasons I started my accelerator program and built a community of some of the world's most talented creatives, was because I saw the impact it had on my life and business. I love connecting people so they can collaborate and pass work to each other, but most importantly, I love witnessing the magic that happens when a group of like-minded people come together for the same reason.

You've probably heard the saying that you are the average of the five people you spend the most time with. This is simply an amplification of that theory. Throughout my life, I have tried to surround myself with people who were wiser and more successful than me, but it wasn't always easy. The people at the top of their game want to surround themselves with people better than them, so the barrier to entry is high. At least that is what I thought until I learned about a secret door to the high achievers' club.

I had read several books by the Australian entrepreneur Daniel Priestley. He had a writing style that really resonated with me and described complex business ideas in a simple, engaging way. Not only that, but Daniel was prolific. He had written four best- selling books and built a multi-million-pound business by the age of 25. He was a highly sought-after business adviser and in 2018, he was voted the number one mentor for leadership in the UK.

At the time I was feeling deflated and lost so I decided that now was the moment to shoot for the stars. The universe must have been listening, as the next day, an email came through from Daniel's mailing list inviting me to an event he was speaking at in London. When I turned up at the event, I was surprised to see him standing at the front of the room delivering the talk himself. I had read so many books by authors that I loved, but few that really resonated the way Daniel's had. Now he was standing in front of me, in the flesh.

After the presentation, Daniel was signing books at the back of the room. As I waited in line, I had this image in my head of grabbing him by the lapels and shouting, "I need you to be my mentor!". After a bit of thought, I decided that perhaps that wasn't a good idea. Managing to control my inner fan-boy, I calmly approached the desk. The words that came out of my mouth next even surprised me…"I don't know how many people tell you this, but your book has changed my life!!" Daniel looked up at me and smiled. "Most people tell me it changed their wife," he replied. I let out a sort of high-pitched Ricky Gervais-style laugh. He seemed undeterred by my overly exaggerated manner and proceeded to ask my name and what I did. At the time, I had a thousand ideas running through my head and as I rambled, I saw him scribbling something down on the inside cover. He handed the book back to me, I opened the front page and it read, "Creative Entrepreneuring".

That book still sits on my shelf as a reminder of the day I decided to commit more time, money and effort into my business than I had ever done before. I'm lucky enough to have been working with Daniel and his team for over two years now. Not only did it give me the strategies and tools to launch my coaching business, but it also put me in an environment where I met people that are now part of my "team".

Surrounding yourself with people that can help you raise your game is absolutely vital. It opens doors that you probably don't even know exist. I'm not saying the only way to do this is to pay, but it is a back door to the high achievers' club. This is exactly why I have a high price tag and a strict invite only policy to my courses and coaching. I want my clients to know that everyone else they meet on the program has the same level of commitment as they do.

Letting Go Of Control

Most freelancers and small business owners I coach aren't short of work. In fact, after we've worked together for a few months, they often have more work than they can handle. This is a great problem to have, but left unmanaged, it can lead to stress and burnout. One of the main things that causes this is trying to do too many things at once, especially if they are tasks you don't enjoy. Myself and many of my clients find it difficult to let go of control of certain tasks in our business because we have a belief that "no one can do it better than me". Or that it will take longer to train someone than if I just did it myself. What is interesting is that when you study the most successful entrepreneurs, they find people better than themselves to run their business. They know that by focusing on their strengths and delegating tasks they don't enjoy or aren't good at, they will be more successful, have more time and more freedom.

In today's social media-driven world, there seems to be a belief that unless you are working 50-hour weeks, you aren't going to be successful. This belief is certainly not helping us to get to where we want to be. All it's doing is sending us to an early grave. I read an interesting book a few years ago on peak performance as I was curious to find out what separates the top performers in the world from the rest of us. What I discovered was that they had the right amount of pressure in their lives.

What I mean is, they knew when to rest and when to work harder. They kept their mind and body in a balanced space between stress and relaxation. In order to create and sustain that balance, they had various ways they could offload certain tasks that weren't aligned to their key strengths. There are three main ways they do this: delegation, automation and elimination. I will talk about each in more detail, but first, let's address the belief that is keeping many people stuck.

A few years ago, I was coaching a very successful photographer who had projects that most people would dream of. From big named sports brands, to the outdoor adventure industry. He came to me because, although it looked like he was successful from the outside, he was burned-out and had a poor work-life balance. When we started to explore what was causing this, it turned out that he was trying to do everything himself. The real challenge was that he believed this is how it should be, and that by letting go of control it was no longer his work.

One of the exercises I asked him to do was to write down all of the things that he did on a daily basis, from getting up in the morning to going to bed at night. It seemed like a ridiculous exercise at the time, but what it revealed was all of the low-value, repetitive tasks he was doing every day. The thought of not doing things himself really didn't sit well, so the only thing I could do was to show him how this was never going to improve, until he let go of control.

When we explored what he really wanted his life and business to look like, we agreed there were two main ways to get there: take on less projects and earn less money or keep the same amount of projects, but delegate, automate or eliminate some of these tasks. He considered both options and decided that the second was best. We just needed to find a way he could do this whilst still feeling like it was his business. In the next section I'm going to share with you exactly how this was done.

Automation, Delegation And Elimination

One of the most valuable books I read on the subject of outsourcing and systemising was *The 4-Hour Work Week* by Tim Ferriss. In the book, Ferriss talks about the power of automation, delegation and elimination, and he gives some great guidance and advice on how to do each one.

Just to clarify, automation is the process of taking a repetitive task and making it automatic. This could be through software or simply by creating a structured process, where someone else can crank the handle. Delegation is about giving parts of a project, or tasks to someone who is either more qualified than you, or where the task isn't a good use of your time (low value). Elimination is looking at the things you can stop doing. I often find that people underestimate how many of these tasks there actually are. Most tasks are nowhere near as important as you think. Being able to let go and decide that you just aren't going to do that task is extremely powerful. It may feel uncomfortable at first, but once you have a system that allows you to decide what isn't worth doing, it becomes much easier.

Let's take a look at automation first. Most people think they have to be some sort of tech wizard to automate things in their business. The truth is, automation is simply about describing a process in enough detail that anyone, or anything, can replicate it consistently and produce the same result. Think about how much time you spend doing the same tasks every week. Things like uploading photos to Dropbox, replying to emails or sending proposals. These are the tasks that are repeatable, and therefore can be automated.

So what is the difference between automation and delegation? Well, it comes down to the process; some things change frequently and therefore you can never fully automate them. Delegation is simply about handing projects and tasks to someone else, whether they are repeatable or not.

There is no way to spend your time on the high-value, creatively fulfilling tasks, if you are trying to do everything on your own. The thought of delegating tasks can seem intimidating as it can feel as if you don't have the budget or don't know where to begin. There are lots of great resources on doing this well without a large budget, including the aforementioned *Four-Hour Work Week*. The important thing to note is that you don't have to build an agency, you just have to find people that are able to do basic tasks. Start small and experiment with simple processes that wouldn't cause your business to fail if they weren't' done exactly how you do them.

When you start to think about yourself more as a business, it allows you to see things in a different light. You don't have to employ people to have this freedom either. There are plenty of freelancers who have small, remote, part-time teams who support them; taking away all of the admin and allowing them to focus on the business and creativity.

Finding the right people to support you is a topic that has filled many books of this size. I won't get into a huge amount of detail here, as firstly, it's not my area of expertise and, secondly, I believe you now have some powerful tools to move you in the right direction. Once you know your values and can work out someone else's, the rest is really just semantics. I've tried to build a team based on skill sets and it didn't work for me. What I have now is a network of people with similar values and goals that want to collaborate and help bring my vision to life. Some of these are freelancers that I pay, as and when I need them, and some are a more permanent part of my team. The one thing I wish I would have built earlier is a support network of people who support me on my mission.

Creating Systems

If you study the high performers of the world, whether it's an athlete or a CEO, they all have one thing in common: reliable systems. They don't just wake up every day and decide what to do; they have systems in place that allow them to keep moving forward, without having to think every option through in their head first. They don't try to do everything themselves (it may look like it from the outside), they have teams of people supporting them. Advisors, trainers, coaches and mentors. People who are experts in their fields and have a huge amount of knowledge. In order to keep everything ticking along, they must have systems in place to guide their team and be as efficient as possible.

In my experience, creatives hate the concept of systems because it involves routine and predictability. There are very few people I coach that don't require a high level of variety to thrive and I am no exception to that rule. If things get too predictable and monotonous, I get bored and frustrated very quickly, to the point where I will sometimes sabotage something because it's working too well. It's really important to be aware of this, but it's also important to create systems that allow you maintain a high level of variety in your day to day life.

Ultimately, variety is about the freedom of choice. We don't want to feel like we have no say in what we do every day. The problem is, having lots of choices requires us to make decisions constantly and we only have a finite capacity to do that. If we are constantly making decisions, we eventually get worn out and have less energy and focus to put into our creative work. There is actually a theory known as 'decision fatigue' which relates to our limited capacity for decision making. Allegedly, it's one of the reasons Steve Jobs wore the same turtleneck jumper every day.

If you want freedom, it's better to create systems that allow your business to keep ticking along, without you having to make decisions all of the time. With these systems in place, you can focus on doing the work you love and saving your energy for high-value tasks. So what do I mean exactly when I say systems? Simply, a documented process and a way that you tackle repetitive tasks on a consistent basis. For example, when you win a new client, you will likely go through a similar process each time. If you document and systemise this as much as possible, it means you can spend more energy and time on the important things.

The best way to create systems is to imagine that you have to give the task to someone else who knows nothing about your business. Walk them through each step of the process from the minute the client says yes to kicking off the project. What are all of the steps that happen and what order do they happen in? It may seem like this is a laborious process, but it will save you so much time, energy and headspace in the long run. When you do come to delegating and automating some of your work, you already have all of the systems in place to make it run smoothly.

Systems aren't just important in business either. I've found that adopting these principles in other areas of my life considerably reduces my stress level and gives me more energy. It could be as simple as your workout routine or what you eat. If you don't have rituals and systems to make these decisions for you, then they are less likely to get done and will take up way more energy.

If you've ever tried to get in shape without a plan and a system to follow, you will have experienced this first-hand. If you walk into the gym and decide what to do in the moment you probably end up resorting to exercises you know or the things you find easiest. You might go to the gym for several months and not really see much progress. However, if you get a good personal trainer and they write out a plan for you with a system to follow day by day, your results increase dramatically. Soon, tracking calories and doing the new exercises becomes second nature. Your brain has internalised them and now has an unconscious system to follow every day.

Choose a task in your life that you do regularly but you feel takes a lot of cognitive energy or causes you stress. As an experiment for the next ten days, write down a plan you can follow systematically for each step of the process. Run through it in your head and imagine you have to give these instructions to someone else. Once you have the plan, don't overthink it, just follow the steps next time you need to do the task. I think you will be surprised how much easier it seems.

The right systems really can free up a huge amount of time, energy and even money in your life and business. Once you have them in place and they are working like a well-oiled machine, it will feel as if things move along so much easier with the same amount of effort.

In the final chapter I'm going to share some advice that I wish I had acted upon years ago.

CHAPTER TEN
NUGGETS OF WISDOM

> "Common sense is the most widely shared commodity in the world, for every man is convinced that he is well supplied with it."
> — Rene Descartes

For the final chapter, I want to share some of the things that I wish I had done differently. Although I have absolutely no regrets, I feel obliged to pass on some of this advice, because it could have saved me a lot of time, energy and money. The hard thing to admit is that I knew most of these things but wasn't doing anything with the knowledge.

Some of it may sound cliché, but that is for a good reason. It's easy to dismiss advice you hear all of the time, but there is a big difference between common sense and common practice. Knowing something isn't enough, we must practice it religiously, no matter how trite it may seem.

One of the things that fascinates me about many of the people I admire, dead and alive, is that they practice/d the fundamentals, consistently. They aren't just full of good ideas, they practice turning these ideas into actions. Take time to revisit this chapter and ask yourself if you now understand the concepts in this book intellectually, or if you know them because you are living them every day. If you manage to turn these ideas into action, they will allow you to have a much smoother journey in the months and years to come.

Discomfort Is the Gateway to Success

At least once a year, I run something called the '30 Day Discomfort Challenge', to help me practice stepping outside of my comfort zone. You may be wondering why I want to practice being uncomfortable and it's a valid question.

Do you remember a time when you did something that felt really uncomfortable? Maybe you did it because you had to, or maybe you pushed yourself to do it. Either way, I bet you felt good after you had done it. Maybe you even felt a sense of achievement and confidence that you hadn't felt before?

Doing things that are uncomfortable feels good after the event, but rarely before or during. The reason it feels good is that it gives us a sense of growth, which, according to Tony Robbins, is one of our six human needs. If you think about it, without discomfort, there can't be any real growth. Growth comes from stepping outside of our comfort zone and facing new challenges. So, why don't we do it more often?

The reason for this is actually more biological than you might think. There is a part of our brain called the limbic system, which is responsible for a lot of our emotional decisions. Specifically, there is a part of the limbic system called the amygdala, which relates to our fight or flight response. Because this part of our brain is primarily concerned with keeping us safe, it doesn't have a very refined judgement when it comes to distinguishing between perceived threats and real ones. That's why you experience physical sensations when you watch a scary film or imagine something dangerous. As we spend a large part of our life imagining future scenarios, we often avoid or resist things that feel uncomfortable. We then have a battle between the limbic system and the prefrontal cortex, which knows logically that the situation in real life is unlikely to do you any physical harm.

The limbic system usually wins this battle, and it takes real strength and courage to be able to fight it. Our brain has good intentions, but it's often stopping us from moving towards our goals and making real progress in our lives. The problem is it often moves us away from things that are likely to improve our chances of success. This could be anything from picking up the phone to a potential client, to giving a presentation to a group of strangers.

Stepping out of your comfort zone is a way to practice getting comfortable with being uncomfortable. It's something that expands or contracts in relation to how much you exercise it. The more uncomfortable you get, the more comfortable those uncomfortable things start to become. If you really want to take your life and business to the next level, practising being uncomfortable is an essential part of that. If you ever feel stuck, just put yourself in an uncomfortable situation and take massive action towards a goal. It will completely change how you feel and get you unstuck almost instantly.

Someone, Somewhere Woke Up Today With Exactly What You Need

Have you ever thought to yourself, I wish I had more time, money, contacts etc? It's a common way of thinking, but is probably stopping you from achieving some, if not all of your goals. One of the key things I've learned over the last few years, working with some very successful people, is that they believe they have almost unlimited resources. The most fascinating thing about this belief is they had it long before they were successful.

They understand that they don't personally have to have the resources to achieve their goals. They focus on finding the people that already have what they need and then creating agreements that are beneficial for both parties. Would your freelance business be different if you could just get in front of more people? Maybe if you just had an extra few thousand pounds you could finally invest in that equipment you need or work with that mentor who is just out of reach. Well, someone has those resources you need right now.

If a friend came up to you tomorrow and asked to borrow £50,000, you would probably tell them you didn't have it. However, if a family member needed a life-saving operation that was going to cost this much or were being held at ransom, you would probably get creative very quickly. It's our beliefs around money and other resources that holds us back more than the resources themselves. I know that might be hard to believe when you don't have them, but I can assure you, they are a lot easier to obtain than you might think.

Think about everything you've had to do up until now to get to where you are. The times you've had to be resourceful on projects and solve problems quickly. You didn't always have the resources, but you found a way to overcome challenges and produce results. Imagine if you amplified those skills and instead of focusing on gaining more resources personally, you got really good at leveraging other peoples'. It's not a lack of resources that is your problem, it's your belief about how you obtain them and your ability to be resourceful.

There Is No Such Thing As The Right Time.

When I first started my career in the creative industries, I believed that there was going to be a time when everything aligned, and it was a signal to act and move forwards. I waited and waited, continued building my portfolio and learning new skills. To my surprise, that time never came and something always felt like it wasn't quite right. I realised that I was going to have to create that time with my own actions and decisions. Things are never going to line up perfectly, there is always going to be something that isn't quite how you want it to be.

I don't want to get too spiritual, but something strange happens when you take the leap before you can see the landing. Trusting that things will be ok and committing to an outcome is the best way I know to make things happen. Obviously, I'm not suggesting you take risks that could lead to dangerous or irreversible outcomes. There are plenty of ways to calculate risks and stack the odds in your favour, but you can't wait for everything to be perfectly aligned.

Fit Your Oxygen Mask First

I see so many freelancers and small business owners who are constantly stressed out and busy because they are at the mercy of their clients. They put the client before everything, including their own health and well-being. What would your business be like if you treated yourself the same way you treat your clients? If you gave yourself the same amount of respect and priority. Would you work the same hours? Would you take more holidays?

One of the main reasons people fail to do the type of work they love on a consistent basis is because they just don't put time aside to work on themselves and their business. It's a like being out at sea on a boat with no engine or rudder, you can't control how fast you are going or what direction; you are at the mercy of the tide and current. If you make yourself as important as your clients, you will give yourself the opportunity to create some space and direction in your life. This can be as simple as blocking out time in your diary to work on your own website or to do some of the exercises in this book. One of the reasons my clients find coaching so valuable, is that it forces them to put time aside to focus on themselves and their business, rather than just getting swept along with the current. Schedule some regular time in your calendar right now to focus on yourself and your business.

It's Hard And It Gets Harder

If you expect building a business to be easy, you are going to be disappointed. As soon as I realised that everyone finds business hard, and that you need to embrace the challenge, it completely changed how I felt. Just because it's hard, doesn't mean it can't be fun. In fact, the more fun you have, the easier it becomes. Challenges are inevitable and if you aren't facing them, you probably aren't doing anything worth talking about.

If you crave the easy, simple life, this journey probably isn't for you and you are better off having a job – something you can just leave behind at the end of each day and not worry about it until you get into the office again. However, if that was you, I don't think you would have read this far.

The really good news is that the more successful you become, the bigger your challenges get. If you accept that challenges are a crucial part of building a successful freelance business, you will enjoy the journey a lot more. This is one of the most valuable lessons I learned from my mentors over the years and it has allowed me to feel good on a daily basis, regardless of what is going on. I see it as an opportunity to solve problems and improve my process. Remember that emotion is created by focus and meaning. When you face a challenge in your business, just ask yourself what meaning you are giving to that challenge and what you are focused on. Are you asking yourself what you can learn and improve on from the challenge, or are you asking yourself why you are so stupid and how this could happen?

I'm not suggesting that we don't have negative events in our lives and walk around with rose-tinted glasses. I'm simply opening up the idea that when we focus on the things that, A) we usually can't control, and B) we believe to be negative experiences, it puts us in an unresourceful state and increases the chance of finding ourselves constantly being in negative situations.

You Are More Powerful Than You Think

Have you ever pushed yourself out of your comfort zone, shot for the stars and achieved something that you didn't realise you were capable of? Most of us have overcome adversity and achieved things in spite of the odds, but these moments are often fleeting. Over the past few years, I've put myself in an environment that has forced me to play a bigger game. I have surrounded myself with people who are building bigger businesses and making more impact in the world than I am and have continually been surprised at what I'm able to achieve.

Roger Banister was the first man to run a four-minute mile. Prior to that, no one had thought it was possible, and many had tried and failed. Not only has the four-minute mile been run by thousands of athletes, but the time has come down by almost 17 seconds. When I hear this story, I'm always reminded of the limitations we put on ourselves and how our world is shaped by our beliefs. The truth is, you are more powerful than you think. It may sound a little bit corny, but you have the ability to achieve things beyond your wildest dreams. All you need to do is have a clear plan, take consistent action and pay attention to what is getting you closer to your goals and, what isn't working. Continually tweak and adjust and eventually you will reach your destination, it's a simple law of averages.

Interestingly, over the past few years coaching some extremely talented creatives, I've found they are often as scared of what they can achieve as what they can't. They find ways to sabotage their success so that they don't stand out too much and people don't become jealous of them. The way I've overcome this is by making success about my clients rather than about myself. The more my clients succeed, the more I succeed, it's as simple as that. As I've said in previous chapters, by taking the focus off yourself and putting in on other people, it will allow you to push through self-doubt and limiting beliefs. Most of us have been brought up to be modest, not speak out of line and to be happy with what we are given. I'm all for gratitude, but limiting your potential so that you don't upset people isn't serving anyone. In fact, I would go as far as to say that it's a complete waste of potential.

Afterword

Congratulations on reading this far and implementing some of the strategies and principles in this book. You are now at the beginning of a new journey and I hope you decide to live your life and run your business differently.

Your values are the foundation of everything you do. They guide your decisions and control how you act in the world. Don't just do the exercise once, make sure you continually revisit and adapt them throughout your life. Once you understand the principle of values, it won't just allow you to feel better, it will also allow you to see why people behave in a certain way. You will start to understand how people are using vehicles to try and meet their values and be able to build better relationships with them.

Hopefully by now, you have realised that you are more than just your skill set or craft. Your story is unique, and it is pointing you towards a real-world problem you can solve for a specific type of person. By solving this problem, you will get greater fulfilment in your work, earn more money and make a bigger impact in the world.

By identifying who you really want to help, you will be able to start meaningful conversations on a consistent basis. You will be able to pick and choose who you work with and avoid the cycle of feast and famine. Having a structured sales conversation with the right people, at the right time, will position you as a guide and help you to avoid being a worker or feel like a creative monkey. Once you realise that people want a specific outcome, it will allow you to package your services into a product that delivers that outcome. This means you create a significant transformation for your clients and can charge more money.

Finally, once you have honed this process, you will build valuable systems that mean you can focus on doing the work you love and spending your time in the most efficient way. Just remember, you are designing a business from your life, not a life from your business.

What next?

Have you ever read a book, watched a video or been to a workshop and had loads of great ideas? Maybe you scribbled them down frantically and filled your notebook. You left feeling pumped up, excited and ready to change your life and business. As the days passed, maybe that excitement faded but you had good intentions to build on the momentum. If you are anything like I was, you probably found that notebook in a draw six months later with very few goals checked off.

I appreciate there is a lot of content in this book and it may seem a little overwhelming. It's my best thinking from more than a decade of ideas, experiences and insights. You don't have to do everything at once, but you do have to do *something*. If you want to turn insight into action, you have to start small and be consistent. I've found there are three key elements that you need to have if you want results. The first is the right environment as I mentioned in the previous chapter. Surrounding yourself with people who are going to push you and help you grow. The second is accountability, which will ensure you are staying on track. The final thing is the correct strategy or framework which you have right in front of you.

The book you have just read is an overview of the whole process I take my clients through in a 9-month period. There are constant iterations, pivots and challenges, but the business and life they leave with is not the same as the one they came to me with. I hope that by reading it, you will achieve in 9 months what it took me to achieve in 9 years. I also hope that you won't try and do this on your own. Whether it's with me or someone else, this journey is best enjoyed with other people.

If you would like to find out more about my 9 month accelerator program where we help award wining freelancers and creative agencies to break through the glass ceiling, work with their dream clients and create financial stability, come to one of my taster workshops and find out if it's a good fit for you. www.mattessam.co.uk/

The program is invite-only and there are certain criteria you must meet in order to be accepted. This ensures we have a high level of success and create an environment of like-minded people that support each other. In addition to the tools and strategies I've shared with you in this book, there are more resources in the form of video, audio and graphics that you can access for free, on my website: www.mattessam.co.uk/free-resources

If you found this book valuable, please take two minutes to leave a review on Amazon.

Acknowledgements

Firstly, I would like to acknowledge one of my mentors, Daniel Priestley, for inspiring me to write this book and helping me to find my entrepreneurial sweet spot. There is no doubt that without your advice and guidance, I wouldn't be where I am today.

Secondly, I would like to acknowledge my friends and family for their ongoing support and interest. I would especially like to thank my parents who have always encouraged me to follow my passions and supported me in whatever path I decided to pursue.

Finally, I would like to thank all of my clients for giving me a sense of purpose and allowing me to have my dream job. For those of you who were test readers for this book and agreed to be case studies, I will be eternally grateful.

About Matthew Essam

Having worked in the creative industries for over 12 years within big agencies as well as running his own freelance business, Matthew realised that being successful was about more than working on big projects with famous brands.

In 2015, a series of unexpected events changed his perspective on life and he decided that it was time to find some meaning and purpose in his work. With the support of some of the UK's leading entrepreneurs and mentors, Matthew developed a framework that he now uses to help creative freelancers and small agencies find work that is both creatively fulfilling and financially rewarding.

If you would like to work directly with Matthew and his team, head over to his website to apply. www.mattessam.co.uk

www.ingramcontent.com/pod-product-compliance
Lightning Source LLC
Chambersburg PA
CBHW030652220526
45463CB00005B/1738